Macmillan Modern Office

922/007

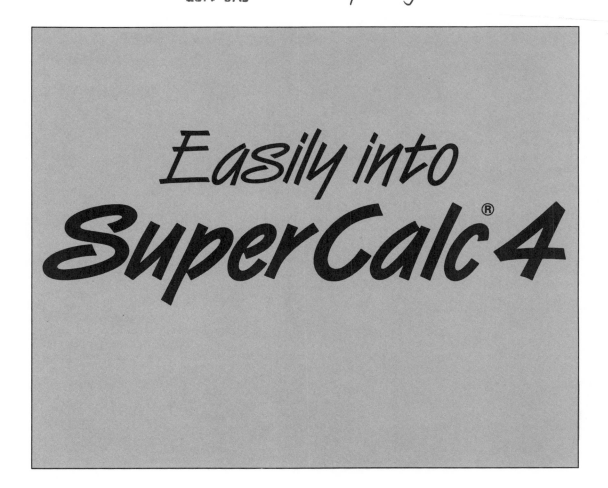

Easily into SuperCalc® 4

Peter Gosling

MACMILLAN

First published 1989

Published by
MACMILLAN EDUCATION LTD
Houndmills, Basingstoke, Hampshire RG21 2XS
and London
Companies and representatives
throughout the world

Printed in Great Britain
by Scotprint Ltd, Musselburgh, Scotland.

British Library Cataloguing in Publication Data
Gosling, P. E. (Peter Edward)
Easily into SuperCalc 4. — (Macmillan
modern office).
1. Microcomputer systems. Spreadsheet
packages. SuperCalc 4
I. Title
005.36'9

ISBN 0-333-47551-8

CONTENTS

Biography   v

Acknowledgements   vi

About this Book   1

What is a Spreadsheet?   2

Lesson One
Starting SuperCalc4, moving about the screen, the prompt
and status lines, SuperCalc4 menus, how to end a SuperCalc4
session with the **/Quit** Command   3

Lesson Two
Entering text, numbers and formulas, creating your first
spreadsheet, the **/Save** command   9

Lesson Three
Loading a saved spreadsheet, the **/Load** command, editing
entries, the **/Edit** command, the **/Blank** command, the **/Zap** command   13

Lesson Four
Printing your spreadsheet, the **/Output** command, switching
off the borders with **/GB**, displaying the formulas with **/GF**, listing the
contents of the cells   17

Lesson Five
The **/Format** command, changing the display of text and numbers,
repeating text, changing column widths, protecting and unprotecting cells,
the **/P** and **/U** commands, user-defined formats   22

Lesson Six
Inserting new rows and columns, the **/Insert** command, deleting
rows and columns, the **/Delete** command   30

Lesson Seven
Copying cells, the **/Copy** command, pointing to cells,
absolute references, the **/Move** command   35

Lesson Eight
Some SuperCalc4 functions: **SUM, AVG, MAX, MIN,
COUNT, SQRT, ROUND**. The **IF** function   44

Lesson Nine
The **/Title** and **/Window** commands   49

Lesson Ten
A further look at printing, using **.PRN** files and **SIDEWAYS**   52

Lesson Eleven
Sorting use the /**Arrange** command   **57**

Lesson Twelve
Playing the "Whatifi" game. Ten examples for you to examine   **59**

Summary of SuperCalc Commands used in this Book   **69**

Index   **70**

☐ BIOGRAPHY

Peter Gosling has been working in computer education since the late 1960s. He was a lecturer at Peterborough Technical College until 1981 when he took early retirement having been Principal Lecturer in charge of the Computer Centre since 1974. In that year he inaugurated the first educational time-sharing service in Cambridgeshire and taught Computer Science at GCE A Level as well as working for the Open University as a part-time Tutor in Mathematics and Computing. For a number of years he was a member of the joint City and Guilds/NCC Committee for Computer Programmer Training. Since 1981 he has devoted his time to writing books on computer programming and software. These books have been translated into Indonesian and Hebrew as well as the major European languages. During this time he has also carried out computer training for a large number of local and national companies. In 1986 he was joined by his daughter, Joanna, who had inherited his enthusiasm for the written word and they have already produced one book jointly for Macmillan Education – *Mastering Word Processing* (2nd edition). This partnership is continuing in the current Macmillan Modern Office series.

☐ ACKNOWLEDGEMENTS

My thanks to Colin Townley for letting me use some of his spreadsheet ideas and to Alliance Computers Ltd of Stamford for supplying a copy of SuperCalc4 for me to use.

VisiCalc is a trademark of VisiCalc Corp.
Lotus 1-2-3 is a trademark of Lotus Development Corp.
SuperCalc is a trademark of Computer Associates International
SIDEWAYS is copyright Funk Software Inc. and Computer Associates

☐ ABOUT THIS BOOK

Spreadsheet programs are among the most useful that are available for your Personal Computer (PC); the others are word processors and database programs. The first spreadsheet program to come on the market was called VisiCalc and was the program that really put personal computing on the map. In the ten years or so since this program appeared, many versions of the spreadsheet concept have become available. One of these is Lotus 1-2-3 which is the subject of another book in the Macmillan Modern Office series. SuperCalc appeared shortly after VisiCalc and has gone through a series of improvements known successively as SuperCalc2, SuperCalc3 and finally SuperCalc4. In this book, which introduces you to the basic concepts of this program, you will become familiar with all the commands that will enable you to create and save a sheet, print it, load a sheet for modification and printing, and manipulate the data stored on a spreadsheet. Finally you will be shown how to play the "Whatifi" game. This is the game you can play with a spreadsheet by saying "What if I changed the value of this figure? What would be its effect on the rest of the figures?"

◼ DESIGN OF THE LESSONS

Each of the twelve lessons in this book will give you experience in using one or more commands available in Version 1.0 of SuperCalc4. The lessons contain a brief description of what the command does together with a step-by step-set of instructions designed to lead you easily into the use of that command (hence the title *Easily into SuperCalc4*). The lessons are displayed in a two-column format where the keys for you to press are listed in the left-hand column and the results that you will see, usually in the form of a screen display, appear in the right-hand column. Most lessons are fairly short but by the time you have worked through any one of them you should feel competent to use the commands dealt with in a real-life situation. The later lessons incorporate commands used earlier - thus enabling you to have constant revision.

The course book is accompanied by a floppy disk. This is your practice disk and you will find that you will be using it constantly. It is a good idea for you to copy the disk and preserve the original. You can then work on the copy, safe in the knowledge that if you do any damage to the disk all is not lost.

As with any well-designed program, SuperCalc4 goes out of its way to help you. Press the **F1** function key and you will be presented with a series of help screens each containing information relevant to whatever you are doing at the time. By the time you have finished this course, and the advanced course in the companion book to this one, you will be in a position to use the manual supplied with the program easily and efficiently.

We hope that you find the course interesting, stimulating and above all useful.

□ INDEX

Absolute references 39
Arrow keys 5
AVG 46

Blanking out cells 15
Breakeven spreadsheets 59–62

Changing column width 22, 26
Changing directory 3
COUNT 46
Copying cells 35–8
Creating a directory 3
Creating an invoice 62

Defining your own
    formats 23, 27
Deleting rows/columns 31
Displaying the formulas 18

Editing an entry 14
Entering numbers 10
Entering text 9
Entry Line 5

F1 function key 1
F4 function key 39
F5 function key 6
Formatting the display 23

Global command 18

Headers and footers 54
Help Line 5
Home key 6

IF 46–8
Inserting new rows/columns 30

Listing the formulas 17
Loading a spreadsheet 13
Lookup table 65

MAX 46
MIN 46
Modifying the output 17
Moving cells 41

PgDn 6
PgUp 6
Pointing 35
Printing a spreadsheet 17
Producing a **.PRN** file 54
Prompt Line 4–5
Protecting cells 22, 26

Quitting SuperCalc 7

Repeating characters 25
ROUND 46

Saving a spreadsheet 11
Setup string 53
SIDEWAYS 54
Sorting by column or row 57
SQRT 46
Starting SuperCalc 3
Status Line 4–5
SUM 44, 45
SuperCalc formulas 10
SuperCalc functions 44
Switching borders on/off 18

Titles 49

Unprotecting cells 22
Using **Point** mode 35

VLOOKUP 64

Windows 50

Zapping a spreadsheet 15

WHAT IS A SPREADSHEET?

We all make lists to help us in our work or in the running of our home. A spreadsheet is nothing more than a series of lists stored in the form of a large "sheet". This sheet is divided into a series of cells into which you can "write" the words or numbers that go to make up your lists. The numbers can be manipulated by a series of simple instructions in order to produce such things as cashflow forecasts, price lists, stock lists or even invoices and bills. By using selections from the large number of built-in functions you can easily calculate averages, standard deviations, internal rates of return and a wide range of mathematical functions.

Each cell is identified by means of its reference which consists of its column letter and row number - A1 being the reference of the top left-hand cell in the sheet. The number of rows and columns that you can use in SuperCalc4 is considerable so that very large spreadsheets can be manipulated.

A spreadsheet program can be of great value to accountants, engineering designers, teachers and even, as the author once discovered, an ice cream company.

In order to use SuperCalc4 efficiently you need a Personal Computer with at least 512 kbytes of RAM, two floppy disk drives or a single floppy disk drive and a hard disk, and a printer.

NOTE: when going through the practical exercises in the lessons, only when you see the instruction (**Ret**) should you press the **Return (Enter)** key on your keyboard. A number of SuperCalc4 commands do not require you to press the **Return** key. You have been warned!

☐ SUMMARY OF SUPERCALC 4 COMMANDS USED IN THIS BOOK

/Arrange command allows sorting of rows or columns to take place
/Blank command deletes the contents of one or more cells
/Copy command allows the copying of the contents of one or more cells into specified ranges of cells
/Delete command deletes one or more rows or columns. Can also be used to delete spreadsheets from a disk
/Edit command allows you to edit the contents of a cell
/Format command allows you to change the appearance of one or more cells. The contents of the cells remain untouched
/Global Borders command switches the spreadsheet borders on or off
/Global Formulas command displays any formulas instead of their calculated values displayed in the cells
/Load command copies a spreadsheet from disk into memory and displays it on the screen
/Output command sends the contents of a spreadsheet to the printer or to a file on disk. If the output is sent to disk through this command it will have a **.PRN** extension added. Such a file can be printed outside SuperCalc using the DOS **TYPE** command
/Protect command prevents entries being made into certain cells
/Quit command leaves SuperCalc4
/Save command sends a spreadsheet to disk. It automatically adds a **.CAL** extension onto the file name
/Title command "freezes" one or more rows or columns to act as permanent titles to the spreadsheet
/Unprotect command removes protection from specified cells
/Window command splits the spreadsheet into two sections that can be scrolled individually

Simple SuperCalc4 functions:

SUM - Sums the contents of a set of cells
AVG - Calculates the average of a set of cells
MAX - Displays the largest number held in a set of cells
MIN - Displays the smallest number held in a set of cells
COUNT - Displays the number of numeric cells in a range
SQRT - Calculates the square root of the contents of a cell
ROUND - Rounds the contents of a cell to a specified number of decimal places
IF - Allows SuperCalc to select one of two alternative entries to a cell depending on a test
VLOOKUP - Provides a vertical table from which you can extract, for example, rates of discount, rates of commission and rates of interest

☐ LESSON ONE

In this lesson you will learn to:

* start SuperCalc4

* move about the SuperCalc screen

* know what to look for on the prompt and status lines

* know what the SuperCalc menus are

* end a SuperCalc session

 ## STARTING SUPERCALC 4

If you are using a computer with a hard disk you should create a separate directory for the SuperCalc4 program. Then you should copy the contents of the two program disks into that directory.

	Action	Result
1.	Key in **MD SC (Ret)**	A directory called **SC** is created on the hard disk.
2.	Key in **CD \SC (Ret)**	A move is made into the **SC** directory.
3.	Place the first of the two program disks into the floppy disk drive.	
4.	Key in **COPY A:*.* (Ret)**	The contents of the floppy disk are copied into the directory called **SC**. The files copied are listed as the copying takes place.

Remove the disk from the floppy disk drive when the copying is complete and repeat the operation with the other system disk.

   To start the SuperCalc4 program from a hard disk system move into the **SC** directory and key in

   SC4 (Ret)

If you are using a twin floppy disk system place System Disk 1 into the disk drive **A** - the left-hand drive if the drives are side-by-side or the top drive if they are stacked one above the other (check if you are not sure). Then key in the command

   SC4 (Ret)

```
PAYROLL - H.W.FAWCETT & CO LTD                        Week No:      27        Tax rate:   27.00%
                                                      Hourly Rate:   #4.50
Employee Hours     Overtime Total       Allowances Tax      Net      Standard Working week    37.5 Hours
Number  Worked     Hrs      Pay                             Pay      Overtime rate:    #6.50
===========================================================================================================
  546     45        7.50    #217.50     #67.80  #40.42  #177.08
  213     32                #144.00     #55.30  #23.95  #120.05
  900     60       22.50    #315.00     #70.99  #65.88  #249.12      No. of employees:      15
  345     45        7.50    #217.50     #50.90  #44.98  #172.52      Total wage bill:       #2,662.88
  543     32                #144.00     #67.80  #20.57  #123.43      Total Tax bill:        #396.20
  231     21                 #94.50     #70.00   #6.62   #87.89
  111     37.5              #168.75     #77.00  #24.77  #143.98      Earnings
  678     40        2.50    #185.00     #80.00  #28.35  #156.65      Lowest:        #94.50
  456     40.25     2.75    #186.63     #89.00  #26.36  #160.27      Highest:       #315.00
  324     34                #153.00    #100.00  #14.31  #138.69
  277     37.5              #168.75    #112.89  #15.08  #153.67      Take-home pay
  288     37.5              #168.75     #99.00  #18.83  #149.92      Lowest:        #87.89
  899     39        1.50    #178.50     #56.00  #33.08  #145.43      Highest:       #249.12
  333     45        7.50    #217.50     #98.80  #32.05  #185.45
  671     23                #103.50    #100.00    #.95  #102.56
```

The allowances are entered manually into column E and the tax is calculated by subtracting the allowances from the gross pay in the previous column and then multiplying each entry by the rate of tax in L1. This calculation is displayed in column F. The difference between the gross pay and the tax due is entered into column G and this gives the net pay. You should be able to perform the necessary amendments to the previous spreadsheet but if you want to see how some of the results are obtained you can examine the sheet called **WAGES1.CAL** on your practice disk.

That is the end of your introduction to SuperCalc4. In the companion book to this you will be introduced to more advanced features of the program: such things as drawing graphs, using the spreadsheet as a database, consolidation of spreadsheets, using macros and using spreadsheets produced by other spreadsheet programs.

 ## SUMMARY

At the end of this lesson you will have learned how to:

1.   Create a breakeven spreadsheet.

2.   Create complex formulas by using pointing and the **F4** function key to create absolute addresses.

3.   Create and complete a simple invoice.

4.   Use a lookup table.

Follow the instructions on the screen, which will eventually look
like this

```
                                        ┌──────────────────────────────────┐
                                        │  SuperCalc4 (tm)  │
                                        └──────────────────────────────────┘

                                        Version 1.00
                                        S/N 5156-0443202, IBM DOS
                                        (8087 not present)


                                        Copyright 1986
                                        Computer Associates, Inc

Software superior by design



Press F1 for information about other Computer Associates products.
Press any key to start.
```

	Action	*Result*

5.   Press any key.

```
        | A ‖  B  ‖  C ‖  D ‖  E  ‖  F  ‖  G ‖  H  |
  1   ▓▓▓▓▓
  2
  3
  4
  5
  6
  7
  8
  9
 10
 11
 12
 13
 14
 15
 16
 17
 18
 19
 20
→A1
 Width:  9 Memory: 123    Last Col/Row:A1
   1>
 READY  F1:Help F3:Names    Ctrl-Break:Cancel
```

At the bottom of the screen is what is called the "dialog panel".
This is divided up into four lines. The top line is called the
Status Line. The second line is the **Prompt Line**. The third and

Example 9: Another example similar to the previous one is shown in its final form in the next illustration.

```
PAYROLL - H.W.FAWCETT & CO LTD              Week No:      27
                                            Hourly Rate:      #4.50
Employee Hours    Overtime Total     Standard Working week    37.5    Hours
Number   Worked  Hrs      Pay        Overtime rate:          #6.50
===============================================================================
   546     45     7.50    #217.50
   213     32              #144.00
   900     60    22.50    #315.00    No. of employees:        15
   345     45     7.50    #217.50    Total wage bill:     #2,662.88
   543     32              #144.00
   231     21               #94.50   Lowest Pay:    #94.50
   111     37.5            #168.75   Highest Pay:  #315.00
   678     40     2.50    #185.00
   456     40.25  2.75    #186.63
   324     34              #153.00
   277     37.5            #168.75
   288     37.5            #168.75
   899     39     1.50    #178.50
   333     45     7.50    #217.50
   671     23              #103.50
```

The critical data is in the top right corner where the rate per hour, overtime rate and standard working week are displayed. The hours worked by each employee are listed in column B and in the next column are the computed overtime hours. A user-defined format is used so that any zero entries are not printed. But note that if the number of hours worked is less than the standard working week then no negative figure is displayed. This means that the **IF** function is to be used. The total pay is calculated from the rates, the basic hours worked and the number of overtime hours. This in fact produces some rather hair-raising formulas, as you will see if you look at the contents of the cells. This is why it is essential to use the /Copy command to reproduce these entries down the columns. Try and create this spreadsheet without referring too much to the version supplied on your practice disk. What you should bear in mind all the time is that you should be able to change the sheet by making changes in one or two cells only; the rate per hour, overtime rate and the standard working week are the critical entries on the sheet.

Example 10: Finally we have an extension of the previous example in which the tax and allowances are taken into account. This means adding three extra columns and a cell, L1, that contains the current rate of tax.

fourth lines are called the **Entry Line** and the **Help Line**. The functions of these lines are:

(1)   Status Line: tells you about the current cell, its reference and the current cursor movement direction.

(2)   Prompt Line: lists the options available from a command.

(3)   Entry Line: receives your entries and allows you to edit them when necessary.

(4)   Help Line: provides short help messages and reminders.

The cell reference displayed on the prompt line refers to the **active cell**. That is the cell into which you can enter data at any time. Watch the arrow beside it and notice what happens when you enter data into that cell in the next lesson.

◼ MOVING ABOUT THE SPREADSHEET

Action	*Result*
6. Press ─⟶ (The right arrow key)	You move one cell to the right. Notice that the cell B1 is highlighted and that the prompt line contains the cell reference - B1 - and there is a small right arrow beside it.
7. Press ↓ (The down arrow key)	You move down one cell to B2. Note that the prompt line now shows this cell reference and a down arrow beside it.
8. Press ⟵ (The left arrow key)	You move one cell to the left to cell A2. Again note the cell reference on the prompt line and the left arrow beside it.
9. Press ↑ (The up arrow key)	You move back to cell A1. Notice that the cell reference on the prompt line is A1 and the arrow beside it points upward.

You can move the highlight in much larger steps than just one cell at a time. Try out the following, but first of all make sure that you are at cell A1. Then:

5

Example 7: Now look at the spreadsheet on your practice disk called **ELECTRIC.CAL**. It is a very simple set of electricity accounts. When printed out it looks as shown below.

```
                   ELECTRICITY BILLS Standing Charge:      #3.45
                                     Price per unit:       #.05
Customer Present  Previous Units      Charge
Number   Reading Reading  Used
-------------------------------------------------------------
    3456    2345    1234    1111   #59.00
    3245    6767    6500     267   #16.80
    6789    3000    3000       0    #3.45
    3215    2134    1678     456   #26.25
    7689    7890    6900     990   #52.95
    3216    4444    3432    1012   #54.05
    5674    9078    3215    5863  #296.60
    6790    5000    4560     440   #25.45
    4432    6543    4321    2222  #114.55
    1218    8001    7890     111    #9.00
    5678    3428    2234    1194   #63.15
    5439     768       0     768   #41.85
    4567    1900     800    1100   #58.45
    3218    2100     780    1320   #69.45
    2222    5564    4356    1208   #63.85

                   Total        #954.85
                   Average
                   Bill:         #63.66
```

Example 8: You should by now be able to modify the previous example so that it takes account of the size of the bill in order to ease the payment. This can be done by using the **IF** function as described in Lesson Eight. You should use the **IF** function in such a way as to print beside any bills that are greater than £100 the words "Monthly" and divide the amount in the Charges column by three. You should try to do this without any help, but if you want to see one way of doing it (there are others) you can look at the spreadsheet called **ELECT1.CAL** on your practice disk. The output it should produce is shown next.

```
                   ELECTRICITY BILLS Standing Charge:      #3.45
                                     Price per unit:       #.05
Customer Present  Previous Units      Charge
Number   Reading Reading  Used
-------------------------------------------------------------
    3456    2345    1234    1111   #59.00
    3245    6767    6500     267   #16.80
    6789    3000    3000       0    #3.45
    3215    2134    1678     456   #26.25
    7689    7890    6900     990   #52.95
    3216    4444    3432    1012   #54.05
    5674    9078    3215    5863   #98.87  Monthly
    6790    5000    4560     440   #25.45
    4432    6543    4321    2222   #38.18  Monthly
    1218    8001    7890     111    #9.00
    5678    3428    2234    1194   #63.15
    5439     768       0     768   #41.85
    4567    1900     800    1100   #58.45
    3218    2100     780    1320   #69.45
    2222    5564    4356    1208   #63.85

                   Total        #680.75
                   Average
                   Bill:         #45.38
```

66

Action	*Result*
10. Press the key marked **PgDn**. Then press it again.	Each time you press it you move the highlight down by one screen. (In fact, the cursor tends to stay in the same position and the "window" on the sheet moves down).
11. Now press the key marked **PgUp**. Press it several times.	Each time you press it you move the highlight up by one screen. (Again, the cursor tends to stay in the same position and the "window" on the sheet moves up).
12. Press the **Ctrl** key and —> together.	You move one screen to the right each time you do this.
13. Press **Ctrl** and <—	You move one screen to the left.
14. Move the highlight back to cell A1.	
15. Press the **F5** function key.	**Enter cell to jump to.** =>A1
16. Key in **IA4000 (Ret)**	Highlight moves immediately to cell IA4000.
17. Press **Home**	Highlight moves back to cell A1.

What you have just seen gives you an idea of just how large a spreadsheet you have at your disposal; just think how many cells there are between A1 and IA4000! And you have not seen the entire range of cells by any means. Remember that you are only shown a portion of the whole sheet through a window that allows you to see twenty lines at a time and fewer than eighty characters across the screen.

This lesson gives you only the commonest key depressions needed to move about the screen. Press the **F1** function key and you will see a full list of all the commands you will need to move around your spreadsheet.

Now is the time to leave this lesson and you do this by using one of the most important keys on the keyboard (as far a Super-Calc4 is concerned) as explained in the next section.

 ## THE PROMPT AND STATUS LINES AND THE SUPERCALC COMMANDS

All SuperCalc commands are started by keying in the / character. On pressing it - there is no need for you to press the **Return** key - you will see a list of the available commands. Press the arrow keys to highlight the command you require. Underneath each highlighted command you will see a brief description of its

This information is held in a table that looks like this

```
0    .05
100  .125
200  .15
300  .2
400  .3
```

This table is called a **Lookup Table** and the function called **VLOOKUP** refers to this. If you load the sheet called **DISCOUNT.CAL** from your practice disk, you will first of all need to list its contents. Remember that you do this by the **/OP** command to display a spreadsheet on your printer. Then press **O** for Options and **R** for Report. Follow this by **C** for Contents.

   Now define the **Range** of the sheet to be printed, Align the paper and **Go**. You will see that the contents of the range A20:B24 have an **H** beside them. This means that they are Hidden whenever the sheet is displayed on the screen and when it is printed out in the normal way. You will also notice that a number of the entries have been protected from alteration by use of the **/Protect** command. The critical instructions are held in the cells D9:D19 where they contain a formula such as

VLOOKUP(A11,$A$20:$B$24,1)

This formula tells SuperCalc to look down the left-hand column of the table and match the contents of cell A11 with a number in the left-hand column of the table, contained in the block A20:B24. If the number in A11 is less than 100 then it returns the number .05. If the number lies between 100 and 199 then .125 is returned. Should A11 lie between 200 and 299 then .15 is returned, and so on. Experiment with this sheet for yourself and note that you can change the rates of discount by entering a new rate in any one of the cells E2:E6. This is why the cells B20:B24 contain cell references and not actual numbers. Otherwise, to change the discount rates it would mean that you would have to "UnHide" and Unprotect the cells before you could change them. You can hide and unhide cells through the **/Format** command. If you feel really adventurous you should put away the listing and create the sheet for yourself from scratch.

Example 6: To illustrate just how useful **VLOOKUP** is you should examine the spreadsheet called **DISC1.CAL** supplied on your practice disk. This illustrates how you can have two rates of discount depending on the status of a customer. They can be of Type 1 or Type 2. This provides a dual rate that is held in a lookup table now stored in the range A20:C24 that is protected and hidden. The customer type number is kept in a new column and defines the "offset" - that is, which of the two columns will hold the appropriate discount rate. If a customer is of Type 1 then the discount is found in the first column to the right of the range column. A customer of Type 2 has the discount taken from the second column. Again you should experiment with this sheet to see how it works and then try and create it by modifying **DISCOUNT.CAL**. You do not need to insert a new column to create the extra space to take the customer type number. Simply use **/Move** to move the block D9:H19 one cell to the right. This opens up a space for you to insert the extra information. Then you will have to edit the contents of cells D9:D19.

purpose. For further information on the commands press the **F1** key. An alternative way of selecting a command is to key in the first letter of its name - they are all different, so there can be no confusion. When you have selected your command you will see that you will be offered either a further series of choices from a subsidiary list or you will be given a prompt telling you what is expected of you next.

```
Arrange  Blank  Copy  Delete  Edit  Format  Global  Insert  Load  Move  Name
Output  Protect  Quit  Save  Title  Unprotect  View  Window  Zap  /more
  2>/
MENU  Sort spreadsheet (entire or partial) by a column or row
```

	Action	*Result*
18.	Press ⟶	You move through the list of commands. As each command is highlighted a brief description of it is displayed at the bottom of the screen.
19.	Move the highlight to the **Quit** command.	You will see that it is the command to leave SuperCalc4. You can leave the command line by pressing the N key.
20.	Key in /Q (Quit command)	**No Yes To** **7>/Quit,** **MENU Do not exit SuperCalc4**
21.	Press N (You are selecting the **No** option)	You leave the command line.
22.	Key in /Q (Quit command)	**No Yes To** **7>/Quit** **MENU Do not exit SuperCalc4**
23.	Press Y (You are selecting the **Yes** option)	You leave SuperCalc and are returned to the DOS prompt.

You should note that any command can be selected in one of two ways. You can either move the highlight to the command you want and then press the **Return** key to issue it, or whatever the position of the highlight you can issue a command by pressing the key corresponding to the first letter of that command. Then there is no need to press the **Return** key. Depending on the position of the highlight it is sometimes better to use one method than the other. You will soon get used to it. You should notice also that as you move through the menu of commands you will see a brief explanation of the use of the command displayed beneath it. If you want a list of all the commands and what they do, press the **F1** function key. To leave the command line at any time, you can always press the **Escape** key.

	A	B	C	D	E	F	G	H
1	==							
2		No. off	Width(mm)	Height(mm)	Price/sq.m	Description	Code	
3	==							
4	1	3	3000	1000	10.19	1010		
5	2	1	2500	1500	11.89	1011		
6	3	2	500	750	9.88	1119		
7	4	1	250	500	10.19	1010		
8	5							
9	6							
10	7							
11	8							
12	9							
13	10							
14	==							
15								
16				CLEERLITE GLASS COMPANY				
17				For all Glass and Glazing Requirements				
18				Unit 7, Saxon Road				
19				Eastwood				
20				NORFIELD NF3 7PR				
21				Tel: (09303) 260880 VAT No. 232 242 56				
22	--							
23		Date:12/01/88		Order No: 10102				
24	Delivery date:23/01/88		Customer Address:J.Walker					
25				:45 HomeGate				
26				:Winton				
27				:Swayford				
28			Delivery Address:As above					
29				:				
30				:				
31				:				
32	--							
33	No. off		Width(mm)	Height(mm)	Area (sq.m)	Price(/sq.m)	Cost #	Description Code
34		3	3000	1000	9.00	10.19	103.84	1010
35		1	2500	1500	3.75	11.89	141.37	1011
36		2	500	750	.75	9.88	97.61	1119
37		1	250	500	.13	10.19	103.84	1010
38		0	0	0	.00	0	.00	0
39		0	0	0	.00	0	.00	0
40		0	0	0	.00	0	.00	0
41		0	0	0	.00	0	.00	0
42		0	0	0	.00	0	.00	0
43		0	0	0	.00	0	.00	0
44	--							
45						TOTAL	446.66	
46						VAT @ 15%	67.00	
47						Sub-Total	513.66	

Example 5: The next example uses a new SuperCalc function called **VLOOKUP,** not to mention a few neat little ways to improve the look of your spreadsheet. Imagine that there is a company who sells certain goods and gives a discount depending on how many items you buy at one time. This provides a discounting structure which is flexible and can change from time to time. The current discount structure is such that for

Orders below 100 items the discount is 5 per cent.
Orders between 100 and 199 the discount is 12.5 per cent.
Orders between 200 and 299 the discount is 15 per cent.
Orders between 300 and 399 the discount is 20 per cent.
Orders for 400 and above the discount is 30 per cent.

■ SUMMARY

At the end of this lesson you will have learned how to:

1. Make a directory on your hard disk and copy the SuperCalc4 program into it.

2. Start the SuperCalc 4 program.

3. Recognise the Status Line, Prompt Line, Entry Line and Help Line.

4. Move about the spreadsheet using the arrow keys and the **PgUp** and **PgDn** keys.

5. Move to any cell using the **F5** function key.

6. Quit SuperCalc4 using the **/Q** command.

7. Use the **Esc** key to leave the command line.

No off	Width (mm)	Height (mm)	Price/sq.m	Description Code
3	3000	1000	10.19	1010

but in row 34 these would produce the following displays

> **3** in cell A34
>
> **3000** in cell B34
>
> **1000** in cell C34
>
> **9.00** in cell D34
>
> **10.19** in cell E34
>
> **103.8** in cell F34
>
> **1010** in cell H34

This means that the cells in the range A34:C34 are exact copies of cells B4:D4. The contents of cell D34 on the other hand are obtained by multiplying the contents of A34, B34 and C34 together and dividing the answer by 1000000, which is the number of square millimetres in a square metre. The result is then rounded to two places of decimals. The formula in D34 would then be **ROUND (A34*B34*C34/1000000,2)**. The contents of cell E34 is a copy of the contents of E4 and the price, shown in F34, is found by multiplying the contents of E34 by the contents of D34. The cells in the range F34:F43 are formatted to currency format. Finally the contents of cell G34 are a copy of the contents of cell F4. The contents of the range A34:G34 are then copied into the block A35:G43. This should be done by saying that you are copying from the range A34:G34 into the range A35:A43.

The total cost of the order is calculated by the formula in cell F45 - **SUM(F43:F34)** - and the VAT at 15 per cent is calculated in F46. Finally the total is displayed in cell F46.

Try this by entering some information onto the sheet and see if it produces a result that looks like that in the next illustration.

NOTE: In the examples you will notice that a # sign is printed instead of a £ sign. This is due to the annoying habit of some printers being unable to give you the British currency symbol and on the printer used to produce these examples this feature was sacrificed in favour of clear, legible output.

☐ LESSON TWO

In this lesson you will learn to:

* enter text, numbers and formulas

* create a simple spreadsheet

* use the /**Save** command

Having found your way around a SuperCalc spreadsheet in Lesson One you are now in a position to start entering your first set of data onto a sheet. In order to do this, make sure that your Personal Computer is up and running and that the DOS prompt is displayed on the screen: which one depends on whether you have a hard or a floppy disk system. Make sure that DOS is logged into the disk containing the SuperCalc4 program and type the command to load it into RAM as described in Lesson One. You should now have the blank spreadsheet displayed on the screen with the highlight in cell A1. Now enter the following text in cells A1 to A7:

	Action	*Result*
1.	Key in **Mortgage (Ret)**	**Mortgage** entered in cell A1.
2.	Press ↓ followed by ←	Cell A2 highlighted.
3.	Key in **EMEB (Ret)**	**EMEB** entered in cell A2.
4.	Press ↓	Cell A3 highlighted.
5.	Key in **Food (Ret)**	**Food** entered in cell A3.
6.	Key in **Car (Ret)**	**Car** entered in A4.
7.	Key in **Pay (Ret)**	**Pay** entered in A5.
8.	Key in **Expenses (Ret)**	**Expenses** entered in A6.
9.	Key in **Left (Ret)**	**Left** entered in A7.

You should note from this that after you have pressed the **Return** key the highlight moves in the direction of the arrow on the status line. If that is the direction you want it to move in, then you need do no more. By pressing an arrow key you can change this. Once you have established the required direction, SuperCalc will remember it.

9

	Action	Result
49.	Press **F4** function key.	+C2*$B$3
50.	Key in -(	+C2*$B$3-(
51.	Highlight cell B9.	+C2*$B$3-(B9
52.	Press **F4** function key.	+C2*$B$3-($B$9
53.	Key in +(	+C2*$B$3-($B$9+(
54.	Highlight cell B16.	+C2*$B$3-($B$9+(B16
55.	Press **F4** function key.	+C2*$B$3-($B$9+($B$16
56.	Press *	+C2*$B$3-($B$9+($B$16*
57.	Highlight cell C2.	+C2*$B$3-($B$9+($B$16*C2
58.	Key in)) (Ret)	0 in C2.

Now copy this formula into the range D3:D32 and then format it to display in currency format. Protect the range C2:D32.

You have now created a breakeven calculation for the sale of coffee by the cup. You should now be able to play the "Whatifi" game with this spreadsheet. You can alter any or all of the costs and the selling price of your product. Remember that you are working in pounds sterling, so that if the price of a cup of coffee is 50 pence you will enter this as 0.5.

Example 3: Both the spreadsheets given so far are fairly simple. The next step is to extend their features. You should now try to amend the one you have just created to include the sale of buns as well as coffee. In this sheet you should be able to find your profit or loss on the sale of, say, 500 cups of coffee and 250 buns per week. If you find difficulty in doing this, you can have a look at the sheet called **COFFEE.CAL** on your practice disk.

Example 4: Another spreadsheet that uses the entries in one or more cells to modify the contents of other cells is on your practice disk under the name of **GLASS.CAL**. Only part of it is there and it is up to you to complete it. The outline provided for you is of an invoice from a glass company. The order to a particular customer is entered at the top of the sheet together with the customer's address and the delivery address. The rest of the sheet involves the creation of the invoice which can then be printed. Remember that only part of the sheet forms the invoice and so only that section is printed.

You should notice that the raw details of the order, which can be in up to ten parts, are entered at the top so that a typical entry line for 3 pieces of glass 3000 mm in width and 1000 mm in height at a price of £10.19 per square metre with a product code of 1010 will appear across the screen as

	Action	Result
10.	Press ↑ seven times.	Cell A1 is highlighted.
11.	Press ⟶	Cell B1 is highlighted.
12.	Key in **185 (Ret)**	**185** entered in B1.
13.	Press ⟵ followed by ↓	Cell B2 highlighted.
14.	Key in **34 (Ret)**	**34** entered in B2.
15.	Key in **145 (Ret)**	**145** entered in B3.
16.	Key in **45 (Ret)**	**45** entered in B4.
17.	Key in **600 (Ret)**	**600** entered in B5.

By this time you will have entered four items of expenditure:
mortgage, EMEB (the electricity bill), your food bill and your
car expenses. Then in cell B5 you have entered your net pay for
the month. Now you are going to calculate two things: your total
expenses and the amount you have left after those expenses have
been paid.

	Action	Result
18.	Key in **B1+B2+B3+B4 (Ret)**	**409** displayed in cell B6.
19.	Key in **B5-B6 (Ret)**	**191** displayed in cell B7.

Your spreadsheet should now look like this:

```
     I  A   II     B    II    C   II   D   II   E   II   F   II   G   II   H   I
1    Mortgage         185
2    EMEB              34
3    Food             145
4    Car               45
5    Pay              600
6    Expenses         409
7    Left             191
8
9
10
11
12
13
14
15
16
17
18
19
20
→B7
Width:    9   Memory: 123     Last Col/Row:B7
   1>
READY  F1:Help F3:Names     Ctrl-Break:Cancel
```

What you have done is to enter formulas in these last two cells
that tell SuperCalc to add together the contents of the named

Action	*Result*

28. Key in
Quantity increment
(Ret)   **Quantity increment** in A18.

29. Highlight cell B18.

30. Key in **100 (Ret)**   100 in B18.

Now format the range B3:B16 in £ format so that all the entries are displayed in pounds and pence. Then protect (use /**P**) the entries in cells B9 and B16.

Action	*Result*

31. Highlight cell C1.

32. Key in
Cups sold (Ret)   **Cups sold** in C1.

33. Highlight cell D1.

34. Key in
Profit or Loss (Ret)   **Profit or Loss** in D1.

35. Highlight cell C2.

36. Key in **B18 (Ret)**   100 in C2.

37. Highlight cell C3.

38. Press **+**   **+**

39. Highlight cell C2.   **+C2**

40. Press **+**   **+C2+**

41. Highlight cell B18.   **+C2+B18**

42. Press **F4** function
key.   **+C2+$B$18**

43. Press **(Ret)**   200 in C21.

Now copy the formula in C3 into the range C4:C32. You should see that the numbers 100, 200, 300, etc. appear in column C under the title **Cups sold**.

Action	*Result*

44. Highlight cell D2.

45. Press **+**   **+**

46. Highlight cell C2.   **+C2**

47. Press *****   **+C2***

48. Highlight cell B3.   **+C2*B3**

cells in the first case and to take the number displayed in B6
from the number displayed in B5 in the second. To show the power
of SuperCalc4, watch what happens next.

	Action	*Result*
20.	Press **F5**	**Enter cell to jump to.** **=>B8**
21.	Key in **B3 (Ret)**	Highlight moves to cell B3.
22.	Key in **180 (Ret)**	**180** entered in B3. **444** displayed in cell B6 and **156** displayed in cell B7.

You should see that every cell that depends on the entry in B3
will change according to the formulas that are entered in them.
Now experiment yourself by changing any of the numbers in cells
B1, B2, B3 and B4. Do not change the entries in B5 and B7.
  Notice that the status line tells you not only the contents of
each cell (not what is displayed) but whether it contains **Text**
(SuperCalc's name for sets of characters) or **Form** (SuperCalc's
name for numbers or formulas).

 ## SAVING YOUR SPREADSHEET

Place your practice disk in drive **A** if you are using a hard disk
system or drive **B** if you have two floppy disk drives only.

	Action	*Result*
23.	Press **Home**	Highlight moved to cell A1.
24.	Key in **/** (Call up command list)	The list of SuperCalc commands appears on the status line.
25.	Press **S** (Save command)	**Enter File Name** **/Save,**
If using twin floppy disk system		
26.	Key in **B:EX1 (Ret)**	**All Values Part**
27.	Press **(Ret)** (By pressing **Return** you are accepting that you want to save **All** the sheet)	File is saved as **EX1.CAL** on drive **B**.

	Action	*Result*
4.	Key in **Rent (Ret)**	**Rent** in cell A6.
5.	Highlight cell A7.	
6.	Key in **Wages (Ret)**	**Wages** in A7.
7.	Highlight cell A8.	
8.	Key in **Electricity (Ret)**	**Electricity** in A8.
9.	Highlight cell A9.	
10.	Key in **TOTAL weekly cost (Ret)**	**TOTAL weekly cost** in A9.
11.	Highlight cell B9.	
12.	Key in **sum(b6.b8) (Ret)**	0 in B9.
13.	Highlight cell A11.	
14.	Key in **Cost per cup (Ret)**	**Cost per cup** in A11.
15.	Highlight cell A12.	
16.	Key in **Coffee (Ret)**	**Coffee** in A12.
17.	Highlight cell A13.	
18.	Key in **Milk (Ret)**	**Milk** in A13.
19.	Highlight cell A14.	
20.	Key in **Breakages (Ret)**	**Breakages** in A14.
21.	Highlight cell A15.	
22.	Key in **Sugar (Ret)**	**Sugar** in A15.
23.	Highlight cell A16.	
24.	Key in **TOTAL cost per cup (Ret)**	**TOTAL cost per cup** in A16.
25.	Highlight cell B16.	
26.	Key in **sum(b12.b15) (Ret)**	0 in B16.
27.	Highlight cell A18.	

If using a hard disk system

	Action	*Result*
28.	Key in **A:EX1 (Ret)**	**All Values Part**
29.	Press **(Ret)** (By pressing **Return** you are accepting that you want to save **All** the sheet)	File is saved as **EX1.CAL** on drive **A.**
30.	Key in **/QY** (Quit - Yes)	You have left SuperCalc4.

 ## SUMMARY

At the end of this lesson you will have learned how to:

1. Enter text and numbers.

2. Enter a simple formula.

3. Save your spreadsheet on disk.

☐ LESSON TWELVE

In this lesson you will learn to:

* play the "Whatifi" game

WHAT IF I ....?

In this, the last lesson in this book, we are going to construct several spreadsheets so that we can play the "Whatifi" game. This gives us the opportunity to use the computer to change the significant entries in a spreadsheet and see what effect this has on all those cells that relate to these entries.

Example 1: In order to get you started, load the spreadsheet called **PIZZA.CAL** from your practice disk. As you can see it is a sheet that enables you to calculate the profitability of a pizza house, albeit with a very restricted menu. It only sells pizzas! It is also quite small, with the cost of rent, staffing and other costs equally small. You will notice that columns D and F are protected, as is the entry in cell B8. These are entries that you do not want anyone to interfere with. The only things you can alter are the actual costs involved, the price at which you sell each pizza and the increment. This is the size of the step in column D. You can go up in any step size you like, but a good starting point is 10.
   Enter figures of 40, 25 and 20 for the rent, staff wages and other costs. Then see approximately how many pizzas you will have to sell in order to start making a profit if they each cost you fifty pence and you sell them at £2.00 each. Then you can vary any of these numbers in order to play the "Whatifi" game. See what happens when your rent goes up to £50 per week. See if you can find out by how much you will have to increase the price of pizzas in order to keep your profit up without selling any more. You will soon realise how easy it is to see the effect of any changes you may make in the costs and the selling price.
   Examine the structure of the spreadsheet, especially the way that the profit or loss is calculated. Note how this makes use of absolute references, with the contents of certain cells being kept constant in the formulas by using the F4 function key. Notice also how the entries in column D are constructed, by taking everything from the increment entered in cell C15.

Example 2: Now comes the time for you to do this example yourself. It is based on **PIZZA.CAL** but involves a slightly more complex operation. This time we are going to sell cups of coffee. First of all, widen column A to 20 characters.

	Action	*Result*
1.	Highlight cell A3.	
2.	Key in **Price per cup (Ret)**	**Price per cup** in A3.
3.	Highlight cell A6.	

LESSON THREE

In this lesson you will learn to:

* load a saved spreadsheet

* edit an entry

* blank out the contents of a cell

* clear all the data from a spreadsheet

In this and all subsequent lessons you will not be given detailed instructions about moving the highlight to the correct cell. You should have enough experience by now to place the cursor exactly where you want it.

   Load the SuperCalc4 program and make sure that the practice disk is in the correct drive: drive **B** if you are using a twin floppy disk system and drive **A** if you are using a hard disk system.

LOADING A SAVED SPREADSHEET

Action   *Result*

1.   **Key in /L (Load   Enter File Name**
      command)   **/Load,**

If using a twin floppy system

2.   Key in **B:EX1 (Ret)** (By
      pressing **Return** you
      select the **All** option
      from the list: you can
      choose the displayed
      values only or any
      part of the sheet.
      Other alternatives are
      given in the advanced   **All Values Consolidate Part Names**
      course in the   **Graphs**
      companion book to this   **/Load,B:EX1,**
      one.)

If using a hard disk system

3.   Key in **A:EX1 (Ret)** (By
      pressing **Return** you
      select the **All** option
      from the list: you can
      choose the displayed

arranged them in price order for each of the chip types. In order to do this, proceed as follows.

	Action	*Result*
8.	Key in /A (Arrange command)	**Column Row**
9.	Press C (Column option - that is, sort on data in a specified column)	**Enter Column; then <RETURN>, or <,> for options**
10.	Key in C, (Column C chosen followed by the options)	**Enter Range**
11.	Key in A2.F34 (Ret)	**Ascending Descending**
12.	Press A (Ascending order)	**Adjust No-Adjust**
13.	Press N (No adjustment of formulas)	**Go Options**
14.	Press O (Options option)	**Enter Secondary sort column**
15.	Press B, (Secondary sort column is B)	**Ascending Descending**
16.	Press A (This column to be in Ascending order)	

You will then see that the sorting has been done by processor chip code and within that by price.

SUMMARY

At the end of this lesson you will have learned how to:

1.   Sort the contents of a sheet.

2.   Sort using more than one sort key.

Action	*Result*

values only or any
part of the sheet.
Other alternatives are
given in the advanced
course in the
companion book to this
one.)

**All Values Consolidate Part Names
Graphs
/Load,A:EX1,**

Your previously saved sheet has now appeared on the screen. If
you want to change the contents of an existing cell you can
overwrite its contents with another entry. However, you may wish
to change only a part of the contents or you may not want to
retype a particularly complicated entry. Using the /**Edit** command
can save you a lot of trouble.

USING THE EDIT COMMAND

Action	*Result*
4. Move the highlight to cell A7.	
5. Key in /E (Edit command)	**From? Enter cell** **/Edit (into current cell),A7**
6. Press (Ret)	**Left**

You are going to amend the contents of A7 to read **Amount Left**.
But before you do this, notice that the flashing cursor is a thin
horizontal bar. Press the key marked **Ins** and see how the size of
the cursor alters to become a flashing rectangle. Press **Ins** again
and you will see that the cursor reverts to its smaller form. The
size of the cursor indicates whether or not you are able to
insert a character at its existing position.

Action	*Result*
7. Press ← four times.	Cursor moves until it is underneath the letter **L**.
8. Press **Ins**	Cursor becomes a flashing block. If it does not, press **Ins** again.
9. Key in **Amount**	**Amount** is inserted before the word **Left**.
10. Press (Ret)	Contents of A7 become **Amount Left**.

You should notice that although the contents of the cell have
been edited, only the characters **Amount Le** are displayed. This is
because the column is only nine characters wide and so SuperCalc
does the best it can. All is not lost, however, since you will
soon see how to widen one or more columns of a spreadsheet.

☐ LESSON ELEVEN

In this lesson you will learn to:

* sort data using the /**Arrange** command

 SORTING DATA

First of all load the sheet called **MICROS.CAL** from your practice disk. It is a list of microcomputers and certain pieces of information about them arranged in columns. You are going first of all to arrange the entries in order of price.

	Action	*Result*
1.	Key in /A (Arrange command)	**Column Row**
2.	Press C (Column option)	**Enter Column; then <RETURN>, or <,> for options**
3.	Key in B, (Column B selected, then the options)	**Enter Range**
4.	Key in A2.F34 (Ret)	**Ascending Descending**
5.	Press A (Ascending order)	**Adjust No-Adjust**
6.	Press N (No adjustment of formulas)	**Go Options**
7.	Press G (Go - start sorting)	

Notice that when you define the range of entries to be sorted, you start at cell A2. This is because SuperCalc does not realise that the first row contains a title and not part of the data in the spreadsheet. As you would not want to include the title in the sorted rows, you have to tell the **Arrange** command to ignore it. You can use any column as the "Key" column, if you wish and you should experiment by using various columns as the "Key". You can sort in ascending or descending order and you can sort text (such as names) into alphabetical order as well as numbers into numerical order.

As well as sorting on the information in one column, you can sort on a secondary key. This means that, in the **MICROS** sample sheet you can sort on column C, containing the code for the microprocessor chip used, and then use the price, column B, as a secondary key. When you do this, you will find that you have collected all the computers with the same chip together, and

Before you go any further you should now save your amended spreadsheet. Notice this time that SuperCalc remembers the name of the sheet and puts it in for you. Because it knows that you have already saved a sheet with the name **EX1.CAL**, it will ask if you want to change your mind or overwrite the existing sheet of that name. Choose the overwrite option; that is what you want to select, because you are going to use the amended sheet later on.

BLANKING OUT THE CONTENTS OF ONE OR MORE CELLS

Action	*Result*
11. Press **Home**	Highlight moves to cell A1.
12. Key in /B (Blank command)	**Enter range, or *graph-range** **/Blank,A1**
13. Press **(Ret)** (This means that you are accepting the cell reference displayed as the cell you wish to blank out. You could enter any cell reference, or a range of cells to blank.)	The entry in A1 disappears.
14. Key in /B (Blank command)	**Enter range, or *graph-range** **/Blank,A1**
15. Key in .A7 **(Ret)**	All the entries in column A disappear.

You have just specified a range of cells, A1:A7, to be blanked. This is SuperCalc's way of defining a range. The start and finish of the range are separated by a colon (:). If you wish you can enter a dot (full stop) instead of a colon (SuperCalc does not object).

CLEARING THE CONTENTS OF EVERY CELL

Action	*Result*
16. Key in /Z (Zap command)	**No Yes Contents** **/Zap-ENTIRE-spreadsheet?**
17. Press **Y** (You are choosing the **Yes** option.)	The complete screen is cleared.

Now quit SuperCalc and you will be in the Disk Operating System (DOS). You can examine the file if you wish by using the DOS **TYPE** command

A>type b:cashflow.prn

or

C>type a:cashflow.prn

To use **SIDEWAYS** you have to make sure that the program, which is supplied on the SuperCalc4 Utilities Disk, is available on the logged disk drive. Then type the command

sideways

and follow the instructions. You are able to move between the various options on the screen that allow you to change the look of the output. Move the cursor with one of the arrow keys to the place where you can choose the size of the typeface. You have a wide range of choices. These are

Normal	**Huge**	**Very Tiny**
Mammoth	**Large**	**Tiny**
Minuscule	**Extra Large**	**Small**

and the one you want is chosen by pressing any key on the keyboard when you will see the options scrolling through the highlight. The density of the printing is either single or double and these are chosen in the same way. When you have made your choice, move to another option by pressing an arrow key. When the highlight is on the name of the file to be printed you can type in its name; **CASHFLOW** is quite sufficient. **SIDEWAYS** knows that it can only deal with files with a **.PRN** extension. Then start the printing and you will see that your wide sheet is printed perfectly - at right angles to the original direction of printing.

SUMMARY

At the end of this lesson you will have learned how to:

1.   Create a **.PRN** file.

2.   Print your sheet out in condensed print.

3.   Put titles and borders on your printed sheet.

4.   Use the **SIDEWAYS** program.

If you had chosen the **No** option you would have been returned to the normal status line and the **Contents** option would clear out the contents of the cells only. Now you should load your spreadsheet again and practise using the /E, /B and /Z commands.

SUMMARY

At the end of this lesson you will have learned how to:

1.   Load a previously saved spreadsheet.

2.   Edit an entry using the /E command and the **Ins** key.

3.   Blank out the contents of a cell using the /B command.

4.   Clear out the contents of the entire spreadsheet using the /Z command.

supplied with SuperCalc4, called **SIDEWAYS**. This program produces
the output at an angle of ninety degrees to the normal direction
of printing and proves to be very versatile.

Before you can send a spreadsheet to be printed by **SIDEWAYS** you
have to produce what is called a **.PRN** file. A **.PRN** file is one
that contains none of the special characters put there by
SuperCalc when it controls the printing. It is a file that can be
printed out, if you wish using the DOS **TYPE** command (see *Easily
into DOS*). To create such a file we use the /**Output** command to
direct the output a file rather than the printer.

Load the **CASHFLOW** spreadsheet and then proceed as follows.

Action	*Result*
23. Key in /OF(Output command, File option)	**Enter File Name**
24. Key in **cashflow (Ret)**	**Range Go Console Line Page Options Zap Align Quit**

The file will be saved as **CASHFLOW.PRN**. This does not conflict
with the original **CASHFLOW.CAL** file.

The rest of the procedure is exactly the same as when you are
printing the sheet on your printer. You have to define the range
to be printed, align the "paper" and then Go for printing. The
only difference is that the sheet is "printed" to disk instead of
to the printer. You must remember, however, that you are going
through exactly the same procedure as with ordinary printing, but
that the sheet you are going to print will now be quite wide (in
terms of the number of columns printed). So you must be careful
to increase the width of your "printout" to the maximum of 255
characters.

Action	*Result*
25. Press **O** (Options)	**Quit Formatted Contents**
26. Press **L** (Layout)	**Quit Page-length Width Left Top Bottom**
27. Press **W** (Width)	
28. Key in **255 (Ret)**	Changes width printed to 255 characters.
29. Press **Q** (Quit Report)	
30. Press **Q** (Quit Options)	**Range Go Console Line Page Options Zap Align Quit**
31. Press **R** (Range)	
32. Key in **A1.M33 (Ret)**	Defines range of the sheet to be printed. You could type **All** if you want all the sheet to be printed.
33. Press **A** (Align)	Printer set to top of page.
34. Press **G** (Go)	Printing proceeds.

☐ LESSON FOUR

In this lesson you will learn to:

* print your spreadsheet

* display the formulas

* list the contents of the cells

 ## PRINTING THE CONTENTS OF YOUR SPREADSHEET

Having created your spreadsheet on the screen, your next task is
to print it out. In order to do this you have to use the /**Output**
command. First of all you should recall the sheet to the screen
you created earlier since the easiest way to print a sheet is to
copy it directly from the screen onto your printer.

	Action	*Result*
1.	Key in /**LB:EX1 (Ret) A**	
or		The saved sheet called **EX1.CAL** is displayed on the screen. The **A** allows
2.	Key in /**LA:EX1 (Ret) A**	you to select the **All** option.

The next thing to do is to ensure that your printer is connected
to the PC, loaded with paper and switched on. Then you can issue
the printing instructions.

	Action	*Result*
3.	Key in /**O** (Select the Output command)	**Printer File**
4.	Press **P** (Select the output to go to the Printer)	**Range Go Console Line Page Options Zap Align Quit**
5.	Press **R** (You are going to define the **Range** of cells to output)	**Enter range (Currently undefined)**
6.	Key in **A1.B7 (Ret)** (You are defining A1:B7 as the range to be output)	**Range Go Console Line Page Options Zap Align Quit**

Action	Result
10. Press **O** (Options option)	**Quit Report Layout Titles Copies Borders Headers Footers Setup**
11. Press **T** (Titles option)	**Auto Manual None**
12. Press **A** (Auto option)	**Quit Report Layout Titles Copies Borders Headers Footers Setup**
13. Press **H** (Headers option)	**Quit 1 2 3 4**
14. Press **1** (1st line of header)	
15. Key in **SOFTWARE TRAINERS LTD - Page # (Ret)**	This displays the words **SOFTWARE TRAINERS LTD** at the top of each page followed by the page number. **Quit 1 2 3 4**
16. Press **Q** (Quit menu)	**Quit Report Layout Titles Copies Borders Headers Footers Setup**
17. Press **F** (Footers option)	**Quit 1 2 3 4**
18. Press **1** (1st line of footer)	
19. Key in **Continued . . . (Ret)**	**Quit 1 2 3 4**
20. Press **Q** (Quit menu)	**Quit Report Layout Titles Copies Borders Headers Footers Setup**
21. Press **Q** (Quit menu)	**Range Go Console Line Page Options Zap Align Quit**
22. Key in **RB3.M33(Ret)AGQ** (Range defined, Align, Go, Quit menu)	

By following these keystrokes you will find that you will print the sheet on numbered pages with a heading at the top of each page. Each page uses the title defined by the /**Title** command and so prints this down the left-hand side of each page. The page number was set as part of the "header" set up through the **Options** menu.

 ## PRODUCING .PRN FILES AND USING THE SIDEWAYS PROGRAM

Now to another way of overcoming the problem of printing very wide spreadsheets. It involves the use of a special program,

	Action	Result
7.	Press **A** (Tells the printer that the output is to be at the top of a new page.)	**Range Go Console Line Page Options Zap Align Quit**
8.	Press **G** (Go - start printing)	**Range Go Console Line Page Options Zap Align Quit**
9.	Press **Q** (When printing finishes, Quit the Output command)	

```
      |  A  || B  |
1   Mortgage     185
2   EMEB          34
3   Food         180
4   Car           45
5   Pay          600
6   Expenses     444
7   Left         156
```

Notice how the borders displaying the column and row labels are printed. It is sometimes useful to print these but you can switch them off in the following manner.

	Action	Result
10.	Key in **/G** (Global command)	**Optimum Keep Graphics Row Col Dep IterS Manual Auto + - Formula " Labels Protect Border Next Tab**
11.	Press **B** (Select the Border option)	

Now print the spreadsheet again, as explained previously, and see how the look of the printed output is improved by the suppression of the borders.

■ DISPLAYING THE FORMULAS

	Action	Result
12.	Key in **/G** (Global command)	**Optimum Keep Graphics Row Col Dep IterS Manual Auto + - Formula " Labels Protect Border Next Tab**
13.	Press **F** (Select the Formula option)	

18

	Action	Result
4.	Key in **132 (Ret)**	Width changed to 132.
5.	Press **Q** (Quit)	**Quit Report Layout Paper Titles Borders Headers Footers Setup**
6.	Press **S** (Setup option)	**Use F2 or arrow keys, any other character to start fresh. (F2** is the Edit key. If there is already a setup string you can edit it with that or by moving the cursor along the string. Press any other key and you will enter its character into a new setup string)
7.	Key in **\015 (Ret)**	Enters a "setup" string that tells the printer to print in condensed characters.
8.	Key in **QRA1.M33(Ret)AGQ** (Quit, Range, Align paper, Go, Quit output command menu)	Quits the menu after printing. (The range will have already been defined when you printed it out earlier).

You will now see that the printing is in smaller type, but your printout is still in two parts. At least it is getting easier to read. In order to improve the output more the only thing to do now is to amend the sheet. You can move the second part of the sheet, the "Actual" part of the cashflow in the range H3:M33, below the first part, starting at cell B37. Use the /**Move** command to do this and then copy the row titles from A3:A33 to the range starting at A37. Now you can print the sheet in two parts. The first is the range A1:G33 and the second the range A37:G66.

Notice that you can enhance your output by putting a "Header" at the top of every page. This is chosen from the Options menu.

Should you wish to change the look of your printout in other ways, you should consult your printer manual - and your dealer if need be - for the use of different setup strings.

You will have noticed that there are a great number of options in the /**Output** menu. By selecting from these you can enhance the look of the output from your spreadsheet and make it even more informative that it usually is. We are going to continue using the **CASHFLOW.CAL** sheet and as you have probably been changing a number of the output parameters, it is better to start from the beginning, so /**Zap** the screen and /**Load CASHFLOW**. It might seem rather odd at this point but move the highlight to cell A1 and use the /**Titles** command to choose a vertical title. You will shortly see why this is important.

	Action	Result
9.	Key in /**OP** (Output command, Printer option)	**Range Go Console Line Page Options Zap Align Quit**

```
OUTPUT OPTIONS MENU: (*Indicates options saved with /Global,Keep)
*Report Format          *Layout                    *Paper
 Formatted     Yes        Page-length    66          Wait           Yes
 Contents      No         Width          80          Auto-page      No
                          Left            4          Double         No
 Titles        None       Top             2          Line-feed      Yes
 Horiz.        None       Bottom          2
 Vert.         None                                 *Borders        Auto
                         *Copies          1          Character       |
 Headers
1:
2:
3:
4:
 Footers
1:
2:
3:
4:
*Setup String (default)                  (Output range is currently A1:B7)

A2              Text="EMEB
Quit  Report  Layout  Paper  Titles  Copies  Borders  Headers  Footers  Setup
 25>/Output,Printer,Options,
MENU  Exit Output Titles Menu
```

Note how you now have a display of the actual contents of every cell that contains a formula. If you wish you can print this out just as you would for any other spreadsheet. This enables you to examine the contents of a sheet for any possible errors you may have made.

Another way of listing the contents of your spreadsheet is to go through the following sequence of instructions.

Action	*Result*
14. Key in /O (Output command)	**Printer File**
15. Press P (Selects Printer output)	**Range Go Console Line Page Options Zap Align Quit**
16. Press O (Selects Options from menu)	**Quit Report Layout Titles Copies Borders Headers Footers Setup**
17. Press R (Selects Report from menu)	**Quit Formatted Contents**
18. Press C (Selects Contents option)	**Yes No**
19. Press Y (Select Yes)	**Quit Formatted Contents**

☐ LESSON TEN

In this lesson you will learn to:

* improve the look of your printed spreadsheet

* use **.PRN** files and the **SIDEWAYS** program

 ## IMPROVING THE LOOK OF YOUR PRINTED SPREADSHEET

In this lesson we are going to examine the additional printing features of SuperCalc. So far you have printed out quite small spreadsheets, but you have not yet attempted to deal with large spreadsheets such as **CASHFLOW.CAL** which you used in an earlier exercise and which you will have noticed extends as far as cell M33. There are ways and means of displaying this on most dot matrix printers. If you have a daisy-wheel printer you may find that you cannot do this part of the lesson. This lesson highlights some of the disadvantages of having a printer with a narrow, 80-column carriage rather than the wider, 132-column carriage.

First of all, load **CASHFLOW** and print it. Remember that the range to be printed is A1:M33; align the paper at the top of a new page and Go.

You will notice that your printout, because the sheet is so wide, comes in several sections. What happens is that there is a default number of characters in the printed width of the sheet. This means that only the first 80 characters in each of the columns are printed. Then the next 80 characters are printed for each column and this is repeated until the entire spreadsheet has been printed. However this means that the sheet is printed in blocks that have to be cut up and stuck together with sticky tape: not a very satisfactory way of doing things.

Luckily there are a number of things that can be done about this. The first of these is that we can print in condensed characters. In order to take advantage of this you need to do two things. First of all, with your spreadsheet on the screen, proceed as follows.

	Action	*Result*
1.	Key in /**OPO** (Output command, Printer option, Options option)	Displays the status of the output on the screen. Notice that the width of the printout is set at 80 characters.
2.	Press **L** (Layout option)	**Quit Report Layout Paper Titles Borders Headers Footers Setup**
3.	Press **W** (Width option)	**Quit Page-length Width Left Top Bottom** Changes the number of characters printed across a page.

```
OUTPUT OPTIONS MENU: (*Indicates options saved with /Global,Keep)
*Report Format          *Layout                    *Paper
 Formatted     Yes       Page-length    66          Wait         Yes
 Contents      Yes       Width          80          Auto-page    No
                         Left            4          Double       No
 Titles        None      Top             2          Line-feed    Yes
 Horiz.        None      Bottom          2
 Vert.         None                                *Borders      Auto
                        *Copies          1          Character    |
 Headers
1:
2:
3:
4:
 Footers
1:
2:
3:
4:
*Setup String (default)              (Output range is currently A1:B7)

A2              Text="EMEB
Quit  Formatted  Contents
 32>/Output,Printer,Options,Report,
MENU  Exit Report format definition
```

	Action	Result
20.	Press **Q** (Quit this menu)	**Quit Report Layout Titles Copies Borders Headers Footers Setup**
21.	Press **Q** (Quit this menu)	**Range Go Console Line Page Options Zap Align Quit**
22.	Press **A** (This ensures that the printer will print at the top of a new page)	**Range Go Console Line Page Options Zap Align Quit**
23.	Press **G** (Go - start printing)	

```
A1        = "Mortgage
B1        = 185
A2        = "EMEB
B2        = 34
A3        = "Food
B3        = 180
A4        = "Car
B4        = 45
A5        = "Pay
B5        = 600
A6        = "Expenses
B6        = B1+B2+B3+B4
A7        = "Left
B7        = B5-B6
```

	Action	Result
24.	Press **Q** (when printing finishes)	You leave the Output command menu.

SUMMARY

At the end of this lesson you will have learned how to:

1. Fix titles onto the sheet.

2. Clear titles.

3. Create a window in your sheet.

4. Move between windows.

■ SUMMARY

At the end of this lesson you will have learned how to:

1. Print the contents of the displayed spreadsheet using the /O command.

2. Switch the borders on and off using the /G command.

3. List the contents of the spreadsheet.

4. Display the contents of the cells using the /GF command.

Action	Result
11. Key in /T (Title command)	**Horizontal Vertical Both Clear**
12. Press C (Clear title)	Clears the fixed title.
13. Highlight cell A5.	
14. Key in /T (Title command)	**Horizontal Vertical Both Clear**
15. Press **B** (**B**oth vertical and horizontal titles)	Fixes the top five rows and the left-hand column permanently.
16. Key in /**TC**	Clears the titles.

Move through the sheet and you will see that both sets of titles are retained wherever you are on the screen.

 ## USING THE /WINDOW COMMAND

You are able to look at two parts of your spreadsheet at the same time by using the /**Window** command. Make sure that **CASHFLOW** is still displayed on the screen.

Action	Result
17. Highlight cell B5.	
18. Key in /**W** (Window command)	**Horizontal Vertical Clear Synchronise Unsynchronise**
19. Press **V** (Vertical window)	Sets up a vertical window at the highlight position.

Notice how we appear to have two spreadsheets in one with two sets of row numbers. You can move the highlight through the current window. If you move it vertically you will see that both screens scroll with each other. This is because scrolling has been synchronised automatically for you. You can unsynchronise them, with some very strange results, by choosing the **Unsyn-chronise** option from the menu. You can jump from one screen to the other by pressing the **F6** function key. The windows are cleared by choosing the **Clear** option. You can experiment with windows and titles without doing any harm to the spreadsheet itself.

☐ LESSON FIVE

In this lesson you will learn to:

    * format the display of cells

    * change the width of columns

    * protect and unprotect cells

    * define your own formats

In this lesson you are going to see how you can make your spreadsheet look better by altering the way that the numbers and the text that explains them are presented. First of all create a spreadsheet that contains the following:

```
     |  A  ||   B   ||   C   ||   D   ||  E  |
1
2             January February March
3    Wages    440      440      440
4    Tips     85       75       98
5    Bonus    12%B3    12%C3    12%D3
6    Total    B3+B4+B5 C3+C4+C5 D3+D4+D5
7
8    Expenses 125      143      110
9    Tax      20%B8    20%C8    20%D8
10   Total    B8+B9    C8+C9    D8+D9
11
12   Net Pay  B6-B10   C6-C10   D6-D10
13
```

The actual display should look like this:

```
     |  A  ||   B   ||   C   ||   D   ||  E  |
1
2             January February March
3    Wages      440     440      440
4    Tips        85      75       98
5    Bonus      52.8    52.8     52.8
6    Total     577.8   567.8    590.8
7
8    Expenses   125     143      110
9    Tax         25     28.6      22
10   Total      150    171.6     132
11
12   Net Pay  427.8   396.2    458.8
13
```

LESSON NINE

In this lesson you will learn to:

* use the /**Title** command

* use the /**Window** command

USING THE /TITLE COMMAND

When you have a very wide spreadsheet, such as the cashflow sheet
used in Lesson Five, there is often a danger that when you are
entering data into the sheet in columns J, K, L and M you have
lost sight of the text held in column A. Luckily this can be
overcome by using the /**Title** command. Load **CASHFLOW** and proceed
as follows.

	Action	Result
1.	Key in /**GB** (Restore the Borders)	Borders restored.
2.	Highlight cell A1.	
3.	Key in /**T** (Title command)	**Horizontal Vertical Both Clear**
4.	Press **V** (Vertical titles)	Contents of column A held permanently.

Move the highlight to the right and you will see that everything
on the screen scrolls except the contents of column A.

	Action	Result
5.	Key in /**T** (Title command)	**Horizontal Vertical Both Clear**
6.	Press **C** (Clear title)	Clears the fixed title.
7.	Highlight cell A5.	
8.	Key in /**T** (Title command)	**Horizontal Vertical Both Clear**
9.	Press **V** (Vertical titles)	Contents of row 1 held permanently.
10.	Press **PgDn**	Screen scrolls downward leaving the top five lines fixed as headings.

Notice that cell B5 contains the instruction **12%B3**, which means that it displays twelve per cent of the contents of cell B3. Similar instructions are in cells C5, D5, B9, C9 and D9.

We can improve the look of the printed output and the display by **Formatting** the sheet. This only changes the way the display looks; it does not alter the contents of the cells at all. Save it and call it **EX2**.

First of all we are going to make sure that the names of the months line up with the figures in their respective columns. The command to do this is the **/Format** command.

■ FORMATTING THE DISPLAY

	Action	*Result*
1.	Key in /F (Format command)	**Global Column Row Entry Define**
2.	Press R (Select a Row to be formatted)	**Enter row range**
3.	Key in 2 (Ret)(Format row 2)	**Accept Integer General Exponential £ Right Left Text * User-defined Hide Default Width**
4.	Press T (Format Text entries)	**Left Right Center**
5.	Press R (Range the entries to the Right of each cell)	**Accept Integer General Exponential £ Right Left Text * User-defined Hide Default Width**
6.	Press A (Accept the format definition)	

Then do the same for column A and align the text in that column to the right. The result should look like this:

```
       |  A  ||   B   ||   C    ||   D   ||  E  |
 1
 2              January February   March
 3      Wages     440     440       440
 4       Tips      85      75        98
 5      Bonus    52.8    52.8      52.8
 6      Total   577.8   567.8     590.8
 7
 8    Expenses    125     143       110
 9        Tax      25    28.6        22
10      Total     150   171.6       132
11
12    Net Pay   427.8   396.2     458.8
13
```

That has sorted the text out. Now for the numbers. As they are amounts of money they should be displayed in money format; that is to say, there should be two digits after the decimal point,

Having created this simple bill, you can experiment with it to see what happens when the cost of the petrol is less than £25. For this situation there is no discount allowed. But as soon as the cost exceeds £25 the discount of 5 per cent is applied.

What the **IF** function is doing is applying a test: **does the cell B6 contain a number that exceeds 25?** If this is true then the cell that contains the **IF**, cell B7 in this case, will display the contents of B6 multiplied by 15 per cent. If the number in B6 is less than 25 then a zero is displayed in B7. The structure of an **IF** function is that the test comes first followed by the number to be displayed if the test succeeds. After this comes the number to be displayed if the test fails.

To make the resulting spreadsheet look more like a bill, you should widen column C and format cells D4, B6, B7, B9, B10 and B12 into currency format.

Do not forget to **Save** the sheet for future reference and **Zap** your screen before going onto the next lesson.

 ## SUMMARY

At the end of this lesson you will have learned how to:

1. Use SuperCalc4 functions.

2. Make SuperCalc4 take decisions that depend on the contents of a particular cell.

even if they are 00. This ensures that the columns of money all line up correctly with the decimal points under one another. To do this the same command is used, but different selections are made.

	Action	Result
7.	Key in /F (Format command)	**Global Column Row Entry Define**
8.	Press E (Select an Entry to be formatted)	**Entry range?**
9.	Key in **B3.D6** (Ret)	**Accept Integer General Exponential £ Right Left Text * User-defined Hide Default Width**
10.	Press £ (Format the range specified in pounds and pence, complete with a £ sign)	**Accept Integer General Exponential £ Right Left Text * User-defined Hide Default Width**
11.	Press A (Accept the format definition)	

Now repeat this to format the blocks of cells B8:D10 and B12:D12 in the same way. Then your display should look as follows.

```
1
2                 January February   March
3        Wages    440.00   440.00   440.00
4         Tips     85.00    75.00    98.00
5        Bonus     52.80    52.80    52.80
6        Total    577.80   567.80   590.80
7
8     Expenses    125.00   143.00   110.00
9          Tax     25.00    28.60    22.00
10       Total    150.00   171.60   132.00
11
12     Net Pay    427.80   396.20   458.80
13
```

You can now make the output look even better by drawing some lines on it. In order to do this take the following action.

	Action	Result
12.	Highlight cell B7.	
13.	Press ' followed by - (Ret)	A series of - characters are drawn along row 7.
14.	Highlight cell B11.	
15.	Press ' followed by = (Ret)	A series of = characters are drawn along row 11.

	Action	Result
22.	Key in .40 (Ret)	.4 in cell D4.
23.	Highlight cell A5.	
24.	Key in '- (Ret)	--------------------------
25.	Highlight cell B6.	
26.	Key in **d3*d4 (Ret)**	**28** in cell B6.
27.	Highlight cell A7.	
28.	Key in **Discount: (Ret)**	**Discount:** in cell A7.
29.	Highlight cell B7.	
30.	Key in **if(b6>25,5%b6,0)** **(Ret)**	**1.4** in cell B7.
31.	Highlight cell B8.	
32.	Key in **"========= (Ret)**	**=========** in cell B8.
33.	Highlight cell B9.	
34.	Key in **b6-b7 (Ret)**	**26.6** in cell B9.
35.	Highlight cell A10.	
36.	Key in **VAT @ 15% (Ret)**	**VAT @ 15%** in cell A10.
37.	Highlight cell B10.	
38.	Key in **15%b9 (Ret)**	**3.99** in cell B10.
39.	Highlight cell B11.	
40.	Key in **"========= (Ret)**	**=========** in cell B11.
41.	Highlight cell B12.	
42.	Key in **b9+b10 (Ret)**	**30.59** in cell B12.
43.	Highlight cell B13.	
44.	Key in **"========= (Ret)**	**=========** in cell B13.

```
      | A  ||   B   ||   C   ||   D  ||  E  |
 1
 2               January February    March
 3      Wages     440.00  440.00    440.00
 4       Tips      85.00   75.00     98.00
 5      Bonus      52.80   52.80     52.80
 6      Total     577.80  567.80    590.80
 7              ----------------------------
 8   Expenses     125.00  143.00    110.00
 9        Tax      25.00   28.60     22.00
10      Total     150.00  171.60    132.00
11              ============================
12    Net Pay     427.80  396.20    458.80
13
```

The ' character is used to instruct SuperCalc to repeat the character(s) you type in next across the sheet. You should practise this until you feel confident in the use of this feature.

Now you should use the commands learned in Lesson Four to list the contents of this spreadsheet. You will see that all the cells that have been formatted to display pounds and pence are prefixed by the £ sign and that every cell that contains the start of the repeated characters contains '- or '=. Such listings can therefore tell you a lot more about the spreadsheet than just what each cell contains.

Finally you can use the /**Format** command to alter the width of any or all of the columns of your spreadsheet. With your latest sheet still on the screen you can proceed with the next part of the lesson.

■ CHANGING THE WIDTH OF COLUMNS

Action	*Result*
16. Key in /**F** (Format command)	**Global Column Row Entry Define**
17. Press **C** (Select a Column to format)	**Enter column range**
18. Press **A** (Ret) (This specifies column A)	**Accept Integer General Exponential £ Right Left Text * User-defined Hide Default Width**
19. Press **W** (Selects column **W**idth to be changed)	**Enter column width**
20. Key in **15** (Ret) (Column A to become 15 characters wide)	

COUNT	Counts the number of non-empty numeric cells in the range or the list. This can take the form of
	a range such as COUNT(J4:J90)
	or
	a list such as COUNT(A2,A5,A9,A12,A23)
MAX	Selects and displays the largest number in the range or list.
MIN	Selects and displays the smallest number in the range or list.
AVG	Calculates the average of the numbers in the range or list.
SQRT	Calculates the square root of the number in the cell specified, for example SQRT(F5)
ROUND	Rounds the display to a specified number of decimal places, for example ROUND(G9*F4,1) will display the number in the current cell, which is obtained by multiplying the contents of G9 and F4 together, rounded to one place of decimals.

USING THE IF FUNCTION

	Action	*Result*
12.	Key in /ZY (Zap command - Yes)	The screen is cleared.
13.	Highlight cell A1.	
14.	Key in **UNEEDA PETROL STATION (Ret)**	**UNEEDA PETROL STATION** in cell A1.
15.	Highlight cell C3.	
16.	Key in **Petrol:Litres (Ret)**	**Petrol:Litres** in cell C3.
17.	Highlight cell D3.	
18.	Key in **70 (Ret)**	**70** in cell D3.
19.	Highlight cell C4.	
20.	Key in **Price: £ per litre (Ret)**	**Price: £ per litre** in cell C4.
21.	Highlight cell D4.	

```
      |   A   || B   || C   || D   || E   |
  1
  2              January February   March
  3       Wages    440.00  440.00  440.00
  4        Tips     85.00   75.00   98.00
  5       Bonus     52.80   52.80   52.80
  6       Total    577.80  567.80  590.80
  7               -------------------------------------
  8    Expenses    125.00  143.00  110.00
  9         Tax     25.00   28.60   22.00
 10       Total    150.00  171.60  132.00
 11               =======================================
 12     Net Pay    427.80  396.20  458.80
 13
```

Now alter the width of column B to five and then change its width back again to nine, which is the default width.

You now have a spreadsheet that contains formulas that must remain unaltered and numbers that you want to be able to change at will.

 ## PROTECTING CELLS

It is a good idea to prevent the accidental overwriting of entries. To do this we use the /**Protect** command. Make sure that your spreadsheet **EX2** is displayed on the screen and proceed as follows.

	Action	*Result*
21.	Highlight cell B5.	
22.	Key in /**P** (Protect command)	**Enter range**
23.	Press . (Causes protected range to start at cell B5)	Anchor cell.
24.	Key in **D6 (Ret)** (Ends the definition of the range)	You have now protected the range B5:D6.
25.	Highlight cell B6.	
26.	Key in **120 (Ret)** (Attempt to change the contents of a protected cell)	**Protected Entry**
27.	Highlight cell B9.	
28.	Key in /**P** (Protect command)	**Enter Range**
29.	Press . (Causes protected range to start at cell B9)	Anchor cell.

	A	B	C	D	E	F	G
1	RATES OF EXCHANGE US$			1.79			
2	FFR			9.98			
3	BF			68			
4	DM			3.4			
5	Lire			2200			
6							
7	--						
8	Stock No	Price #	US$	FFR	BF	DM	Lire
9	--						
10	A132R	125.00	223.75	1247.50	8500	425.00	275000
11	A143F	34.75	62.20	346.81	2363	118.15	76450
12	A564E	12.50	22.38	124.75	850	42.50	27500
13	B786T	90.00	161.10	898.20	6120	306.00	198000
14	B566F	456.00	816.24	4550.88	31008	1550.40	1003200
15	C777D	43.80	78.40	437.12	2978	148.92	96360
16	C987T	34.33	61.45	342.61	2334	116.72	75526
17	C999X	21.00	37.59	209.58	1428	71.40	46200
18	D321W	10.99	19.67	109.68	747	37.37	24178
19	D555D	33.75	60.41	336.83	2295	114.75	74250
20	D990H	78.90	141.23	787.42	5365	268.26	173580

SUM is one of the many SuperCalc functions available to you. Others that are easy to use are **MAX, MIN, AVG, SQRT, COUNT** and **ROUND**. They will give you the largest number in a range, the smallest number in a range or the average of a range of numbers, count the number of numbers in a range, calculate a square root, and round the display of a number to a specified number of decimal places.

Action	*Result*
9. Key in /ZY (Zap command -Yes)	The screen is cleared.
10. Key in /LA:FUNCTION (Ret) A	
or	
11. Key in /LB:FUNCTION (Ret) A	Sheet called **FUNCTION.CAL** is displayed on the screen.

Examine the contents of the block of cells B14:B20. You will see the use of several of the large range of SuperCalc functions.

NOTES ON THESE FUNCTIONS

SUM Totals the contents of the cells listed in brackets. This can take the form of

a range such as SUM(B3:B23)

or

a list such as SUM(B3,B5,B7,B9,B11)

45

Action	Result
30. Key in **D12 (Ret)** (Ends the definition of the range)	You have now protected the range B9:D12.
31. Key in **/Z** (**Z**ap the screen)	Screen clears.

 ## DEFINING YOUR OWN FORMATS

Now for some more sophisticated formatting because apart from the format options supplied by SuperCalc there are a number of formats that you can define for yourself. In order to practise this type of formatting you are going to use the sheet called **CASHFLOW.CAL** supplied on your practice disk.

Action	Result
32. Key in **/LA:CASHFLOW (Ret) A**	
or	
33. Key in **/LB:CASHFLOW (Ret) A**	**CASHFLOW** sheet appears on the screen. Notice how it has been saved without any borders.

Move the highlight about the screen so that you can see the extent of the sheet and what it sets out to show.

Action	Result
34. Key in **/F** (Format command)	**Global Column Row Entry Define**
35. Press **D** (Define your own formats)	The User-defined options screen is displayed.

This screen allows you to define up to eight additional formats that usually, but not always, are used to refer to the display of financial information. The options available are:

Floating £	Can be **Y** or **N** and places a £ sign before the number displayed.
Embedded commas	Can be **Y** or **N** and separates thousands from hundreds by commas and millions from thousands.
Minus in ( )	Can be **Y** or **N** and places negative numbers in brackets (accountant style).
Zero as blank	Can be **Y** or **N** and will not print zero entries.

☐ LESSON EIGHT

In this lesson you will learn to:

* use the SuperCalc functions: **SUM, AVG, MAX, MIN, COUNT, SQRT, ROUND.**

* use the **IF** function

So far our spreadsheets have been fairly simple to construct, from the arithmetic point of view anyway. But now we are going to be more adventurous and use some of the functions that SuperCalc provides. You will soon see that they can make life very easy for us. First of all, load the spreadsheet you have saved under the name of **EX3.CAL**.

■ SOME SUPERCALC FUNCTIONS

	Action	*Result*
1.	Highlight cell H2.	
2.	Key in **Total (Ret)**	**Total** appears in cell H2.
3.	Highlight cell H3.	
4.	Key in **SUM(**	**SUM(**
5.	Highlight cell B3.	**SUM(B3**
6.	Press .	Anchor cell.
7.	Highlight cell G3.	**SUM(B3:G3**
8.	Key in) **(Ret)**	**SUM(B3:G3)** entered into H3; **2680** displayed.

Now copy this formula into the range H4:H6 and then into H8:H10 and finally into cell H12. Your complete spreadsheet should look like this:

%	Can be **Y** or **N** and multiplies the number by 100 and places a % sign after it.
Decimal places	Defines the number of figures after the decimal point.
Scaling factor	Defines the power of 10 by which to divide the number in order to scale it down. For example, place **3** here and the formatted entries are divided by 1000 (10 to the power of 3).

	Action	*Result*
36.	By using the arrow keys ensure that column 1 of this display defines a floating pound sign, embedded commas, minus in ( ), zero as a blank, no % sign, 2 decimal places and a zero scaling factor.	**1** **Y** **Y** **Y** **Y** **N** **2** **0**
37.	Press **Esc** (Takes you out of the User-defined Format screen)	**Global Column Row Entry Define**
38.	Press **E** (Select an Entry to be formatted)	**Enter range**
39.	Key in **B6.M27 (Ret)** (Defines the range of cells to be formatted)	**Accept Integer General Exponential £ Right Left Text * User-defined Hide Default Width**
40.	Key in **U1 (Ret)** (Selects User-defined Format 1)	The defined block is displayed in User-defined format 1.

Now display the block B29:M32 in the same format. Then save the new sheet onto disk under the name of **CASH1**. You will need it later when we examine further details of the /**Output** command.

◼ SUMMARY

At the end of this lesson you will have learned how to:

1.   Use **POINT** mode.

2.   Copy one or more cells to another part of the sheet.

3.   Create and use absolute cell references.

◼ SUMMARY

At the end of this lesson you will have learned how to:

1. Format the display of cells.

2. Repeat characters across cells in order to draw horizontal lines.

3. Change the width of one or more columns.

4. Protect cells from accidental entry or editing.

5. Define your own formats.

Action	Result
68. Highlight cell A1.	
69. Key in /M (Move command)	**Block Row Column**
70. Press C (Column(s) to be moved)	**Enter column range.**
71. Press (Ret) (Move current column)	**To ? (Enter column)**
72. Press H (Ret)	The contents of column A are moved to column H. Column A disappears.
73. Highlight cell A2.	
74. Key in /M (Move command)	**Block Row Column**
75. Press R (Row(s) to be moved)	**Enter row range**
76. Press (Ret) (Move current row)	**To ? (Enter row)**
77. Key in 14 (Ret)	The contents of row 2 are moved to row 14. Row 2 disappears.

Now you should be able to return the moved column and row to their original positions by asking for the contents of column H to be moved to column A (that is quite correct - even though column A is occupied). Similarly, you can move the contents of row 14 back to row 2, even though that row is occupied. You will notice that SuperCalc inserts a new row or column as required.

Action	Result
78. Highlight cell B3.	
79. Key in /M (Move command)	**Block Row Column**
80. Press B (Block to be moved)	**From? (Enter Range)**
81. Key in B3.D6 (Ret)	**To? (Enter Cell)**
82. Key in A14 (Ret)	The block of cells has been moved and a blank space left in their place.

Notice that the formulas have been adjusted to take account of the new position of the block. Now you should be able to move the block back to its original position.

LESSON SIX

In this lesson you will learn to:

* insert new rows and columns

* delete rows and columns

■ INSERTING NEW ROWS AND COLUMNS

Another change you can make to a SuperCalc spreadsheet is to insert one or more extra rows or columns. You can also insert blank blocks into your spreadsheet. Whenever insertion takes place you will cause parts of the existing data to be moved about, as you will see.

Action	*Result*
1. Key in /LA:EX2 (Ret) A	
or	
2. Key in /LB:EX2 (Ret) A	Spreadsheet called **EX2.CAL** is loaded and displayed on the screen.
3. Move highlight to cell A3.	
4. Key in /I (Insert rows, columns or blocks into the sheet)	**Row Column Block**
5. Press **R (Ret)** (Selects an extra **Row** to be inserted at the current cursor position)	All the rows from row 3 downward move down by one row.
6. Key in /GF (Global command, Formula display option)	Note that the formulas have been adjusted.
7. Move highlight to B4.	
8. Key in /I (Insert rows, columns or blocks)	**Row Column Block**
9. Press **C (Ret)** (Selects an extra **Column** to be inserted at the current cursor position)	All the columns to the right of column B move one column to the right. Again the formulas are adjusted.

	Action	*Result*
50.	Highlight cell B3.	
51.	Key in +	+ appears on prompt line.
52.	Highlight cell A3.	+A3 on prompt line.
53.	Key in *	+A3* on prompt line.
54.	Highlight cell A1.	+A3*A1 on prompt line.
55.	Press (Ret)	+A3*A1 entered into cell B3.
56.	Key in /C (Copy command)	**From?Enter range or *graph-range**
57.	Highlight cell B3.	
58.	Press (Ret)	**To? (Enter Cell);then <RETURN> or <,> for options**
59.	Highlight cell B4.	
60.	Press .	Anchor cell.
61.	Highlight cell B12 - **DO NOT PRESS THE RETURN KEY!**	
62.	Press ,	**No-Adjust Ask Values + - * /**
63.	Press A (Ask for adjustments)	**Source cell B3. Adjust A3 (Y or N)?**
64.	Press Y (Yes - adjust A3)	**Source cell B3. Adjust A1 (Y or N)?**
65.	Press N (No adjustment to A1)	The copying takes place correctly.

What SuperCalc is asking you is whether or not a particular cell
reference is to be adjusted as it is copied. In this example it
is the reference to cell A1 that must remain unchanged during the
copying. The reference to B3 must, however, be adjusted so that
the reference is always to the cell to the left of the current cell.

 ## MOVING BLOCKS OF CELLS

Rows, columns or blocks of cells may be moved about the spreadsheet and this is done using the /**Move** command.

	Action	*Result*
66.	Key in /**LA:EX3** (Ret) **A**	
	or	
67.	Key in /**LB:EX3** (Ret) **A**	Spreadsheet **EX3.CAL** is displayed.

	A	B	C	D	E	F
1						
2			January	February	March	
3						
4		Wages	440	440	440	
5		Tips	85	75	98	
6		Bonus	12%C4	12%D4	12%E4	
7		Total	C4+C5+C6	D4+D5+D6	E4+E5+E6	
8						
9		Expenses	125	143	110	
10		Tax	20%C9	20%D9	20%E9	
11		Total	C9+C10	D9+D10	E9+E10	
12						
13		Net Pay	C7-C11	D7-D11	E7-E11	
14						

	Action	Result
10.	Move highlight to C4.	
11.	Key in **/I** (Insert command)	**Row Column Block**
12.	Press **B** (Select to insert a **B**lock of cells)	**Enter Range**
13.	Press **.** (Fixes start of block at C4)	Anchor cell.
14.	Move highlight to E4 and then to E7.	Notice that the block C4:D9 is highlighted.
15.	Press **(Ret)** (Defines a new block of empty cells to be placed in range C4:E7)	**Down Right**
16.	Press **D** (Select that the existing cells be pushed **D**own)	An empty block is opened up and the highlighted block is moved down.

Apart from showing how to insert new columns, rows and blocks into your spreadsheet, you have just seen how to use a technique called "pointing" to reference groups of cells. This is something that you are going to use a lot in the future. You should now practise inserting rows, columns and blocks into your sheet.

DELETING ROWS AND COLUMNS

Your spreadsheet now looks very different from what it did at at the start of this lesson. You can return to where you were by using the **/Delete** command. Leave the sheet as it is and proceed as follows.

You should now be able to enter, by using pointing and the **F4** function key, the formulas **+B10*\$D\$2**, **+B10*\$D\$3**, **+B10*\$D\$4** and **+B10*\$D\$5** in cells D10:G10. Then you can copy them.

	Action	*Result*
37.	Highlight cell D10.	
38.	Key in /C (Copy command)	**From? Enter range or *graph-range**
39.	Press . (Defines start of range to be copied from as D10)	Anchor cell.
40.	Highlight cell G10.	
41.	Press **(Ret)** (Defines range to be copied as D10:G10)	**To? (Enter Cell);then <RETURN> or <,> for options**
42.	Highlight cell D20.	
43.	Press . (Defines start of target range as D20)	Anchor cell.
44.	Highlight cell G20.	
45.	Press **(Ret)**	Copying takes place into range.

You should check to see that your spreadsheet now looks the same as the one supplied. The only difference you should find is in the formatting of the display of the currency. You will see that columns B:D and F are formatted to show two decimal places while the other two are formatted as integers (whole numbers) because subdivisions of the currencies are not used.

You may have wondered what the options are that are mentioned when you get to the **To** part of the copying. They actually provide an alternative method of using absolute references in copying.

The method described above is in fact the latest addition to the features of SuperCalc4. It is exactly the same method as is used in the Lotus 1-2-3 spreadsheet. All the previous versions of SuperCalc use a slightly more complicated way of doing it. It works like this.

	Action	*Result*
46.	Key in /**ZY** (**Z**ap command - **Y**)	Clear screen.
47.	Highlight cell A1.	
48.	Key in **12 (Ret)**	**12** in cell A1.
49.	Enter the numbers 1 to 10 in cells A3:A12.	

Action	Result

17. Move highlight to A3.

18. Key in /D (Delete command)

Row Column Block File

19. Press **R (Ret)** (Choose to delete the current **Row**)

The row containing the highlight disappears and all the rows below it move up by one.

20. Move highlight to B39. (You will probably already be there!)

21. Key in /D (Delete command)

Row Column Block File

22. Press **C (Ret)** (Choose to delete the current **Column**)

The column containing the highlight disappears and all the rows to its right move to the right.

23. Move highlight to B3.

24. Key in /D (Delete command)

Row Column Block File

25. Press **B (Ret)** (Choose to delete a **Block**)

26. Press . (Start point of block to be deleted is cell B3)

Anchor cell.

27. Move highlight to D6.

28. Press **(Ret)** (Defines block to be deleted as B3:D6)

Up Left

29. Press **U** (Forces cells below deleted block to move **Up**)

Note how the empty block is removed and the spreadsheet resumes its original form.

If you were to choose the **File** option after you had given the /Delete command you would be able to delete a spreadsheet stored on a disk.

Action	Result

30. Key in /DF (Delete command, File delete)

You could type in the name of the file you wish to delete or examine the list of files stored on the current disk: look at the note along the bottom of the screen.

USING ABSOLUTE REFERENCES

If you look carefully at the contents of the partial columns
C10:C20, D10:D20, E10:E20, F10:F20 and G10:G20 you will notice
that they each refer to one particular cell (the one containing
their currency rate of exchange) and then the cell in their row
of column **B** (the price in pounds sterling). Note: the cell B8
contains a # symbol. This is because you will find that most
printers need to be sent that symbol in order to print a £ sign.
Your task in this part of the lesson is to reproduce this
spreadsheet in the most economical way. Obviously the key numbers
are in cells D1:D5 and B10:B20. They are the rates of exchange
and the cost in pounds sterling. Notice that the entry in C10 is
B10*D1, the entry in D10 is **B10*D2**, and so on. So it looks as if
you could simply copy these formulas down the columns. Try it and
see what happens. That's right! Chaos! If you look down the
columns you will see that only the entries in row 10 are correct,
all the others have been adjusted. This is because of the way
that SuperCalc operates. If you enter **B10*D1** in cell C10, what it
is actually saying is "multiply the number immediately to my left
by the number in the cell nine rows above me and one column to my
right." That is, in fact, the instruction that will be copied
down the column. By the time it has reached cell C20 the
instruction has become **B20*D11**. This instruction has now become
totally different from what you intended it to be, which was
B20*D1. There are two ways of doing this properly. The first is
probably the easier and it goes like this:

	Action	Result
	Action	*Result*
31.	Highlight cell C10.	
32.	Press **+**	
33.	Highlight cell B10.	**+B10** appears on the prompt line and **POINT** appears at the bottom line of the screen.
34.	Press *****	**+B10*** appears on the prompt line.
35.	Highlight cell D1 and press function key **F4**	**+B10*$D$1** appears on the prompt line.
36.	Press **(Ret)**	**+B10*$D$1** entered into cell C10.

The **F4** function key is known as the **Abs** key. It causes **$** signs to
be placed before the column letter and the row number. This
creates an **Absolute reference** that cannot be changed by copying.
   Now copy the entry in C10 down the column from C11 to C20 and
you will find that the entries in that column are what you really
need, namely **+B10*$D$1**, **+B11*$D$1**, **+B12*$D$1**, and so on. The
effect of the dollar signs in front of a row letter and column
number force it to remain unchanged during copying. Cell references that contain these dollar signs are described as being
"Absolute" references, while other references are "Relative" as
was described earlier.

Action   *Result*

31. Press **F3** to see the
     screen display as
     shown in the next
     illustration.

```
FILE LIST
Directory displayed is B:\
Data directory is B:\
┌────────────────────────────────────────────────────────────────────────────┐
│ *.CAL                                                                        │
└────────────────────────────────────────────────────────────────────────────┘
<DIECTORIES>   APEX      .cal   ASSET     .cal   ASSET99 .cal   CARS     .cal
CASH1    .cal   CASH2     .cal   CASHFLOW.cal   CLUB     .cal   COFFEE   .cal
CURRENCY.cal   DATES     .cal   DISC1     .cal   DISCOUNT.cal   ELECT1   .cal
ELECTRIC.cal   EX1       .cal   EX2       .cal   EX3       .cal   FUNCTION.cal
GLASS    .cal   GLASS1    .cal   GRAPH     .cal   GRAPHS1 .cal   GRAPHS2 .cal
GRAPHS3 .cal   GRAPHS4 .cal   HILO      .cal   MACRO1   .cal   MACRO2  .cal
MACRO99 .cal   MICROS    .cal   NAMES     .cal   NOREAST .cal   NORWEST .cal
PIZZA    .cal   POLL      .cal   SALES     .cal   SALESMEN.cal   SOUTH    .cal
TOWNS99 .cal   WAGES     .cal   WAGES1   .cal   WEST      .cal




Select <DIRECTORIES> to list subdirectories              1024 bytes free
 21>/Delete,File,ex2.CAL
FILE   F2:Edit F4:Update data directory F6:Toggle details
```

Action   *Result*

32. To change the name of   This moves the cursor to the block at
     the directory whose   the top. Type in the name of the
     files you are invest-   drive, and directory, you wish to
     igating, press **F4**   examine - such as **C:\sc (Ret)**

33. Press **F6**   The list of files will be presented
                                    in more detail.

34. Press **F1** (The Help   You will be given help, should you
     key)   require it, about using these
                                    screens.

35. Press the **Esc** key to
     leave the Help screen.

36. Move the highlight
     from name to name
     using the arrow keys
     to select the file to
     be deleted.

37. If you change your
     mind and wish to leave
     the screen, press **Esc**

	A	B	C
1	100	110	
2	110	121	
3	120	132	
4	130	143	
5	140	154	
6	150	165	
7	160	176	
8	170	187	
9	180	198	
10	190	209	
11	200	220	
12	210	231	
13	220	242	
14	230	253	
15	240	264	
16	250	275	
17	260	286	
18	270	297	
19	280	308	
20	290	319	

Repeat this by heading column C with the formula **115%B1**. You should now be able to produce the spreadsheet provided on the practice disk under the name of **POLL.CAL**. Load this spreadsheet from the practice disk, having first of all **Z**apped the screen. You will see that it consists of five blocks of data, all constructed in the same way. Output the display onto your printer and see if you can create the same screen. In order to do this you have to create the first five rows of text and then draw the line across the sheet ('-). Next you create the block A7:E10. Look at the contents of the cells so you can see how the entries in B10:D10 and E8:E10 are constructed. Then you can copy the entire block into the area beneath it four times. Then all you need do is to change certain items of text and data, and the sheet is complete. You should find that the ease and speed with which you can do this is surprising.

   You should note that you have been copying the contents of a block of cells into another block, but all you have to do is specify the range of the block to be moved and the top left-hand corner only of its destination.

   This is not, however, all there is about copying. Sometimes you have no need to replicate formulas in quite the way described earlier in this lesson. For example, **Z**ap the screen and load the sheet called **CURRENCY** from your practice disk.

	A	B	C	D	E	F	G	H
1								
2		January	February	March	April	May	June	Total
3	Wages	440	440	440	440	460	460	2680
4	Tips	85	75	98	90	88	95	531
5	Bonus	52.8	52.8	52.8	52.8	55.2	55.2	321.6
6	Total	577.8	567.8	590.8	582.8	603.2	610.2	3532.6
7		---
8	Expenses	125	143	110	126	130	150	784
9	Tax	25	28.6	22	25.2	26	30	156.8
10	Total	150	171.6	132	151.2	156	180	940.8
11		===
12	Net Pay	427.8	396.2	458.8	431.6	447.2	430.2	2591.8

You will also find that when you wish to load a SuperCalc file from disk you can select it in exactly this way; so that if you do forget the name of a particular file, you can see them all displayed for you by using /**Load** followed by the **F3** function key. The list of available files will be displayed and you can select the one you wish to load by moving through the list by means of one of the arrow keys.

SUMMARY

At the end of this lesson you will have learned how to:

1.   Insert new rows and columns.

2.   Delete rows and columns.

3.   Delete a file from disk.

	Action	*Result*

17. Highlight cell A2 .

18. Press **(Ret)**
(Defines cell to be
copied)

To?(Enter Cell); then <RETURN> or
<,> for options

19. Highlight cell A3.

20. Press . (Defines start
of range to be copied
into as A3)

Anchor cell.

21. Highlight cell A20.

22. Press **(Ret)** (Defines
the end of the range)

The formula is copied into the range
A3:A20.

	A
1	100
2	110
3	120
4	130
5	140
6	150
7	160
8	170
9	180
10	190
11	200
12	210
13	220
14	230
15	240
16	250
17	260
18	270
19	280
20	290

23. Highlight cell B1.

24. Key in **110%A1 (Ret)**

110 in B1.

25. Key in **/C (Copy
command)**

From? Enter range or *graph-range

26. Highlight cell B1 and
Press **(Ret)** (Copies
from B1)

**To?(Enter Cell); then <RETURN> or
<,> for options**

27. Highlight cell B2.

28. Press . (Defines start
of target range as B2)

Anchor cell.

29. Highlight cell B20.

30. Press **(Ret)**

Copies formula into range B2:B20.

☐ LESSON SEVEN

In this lesson you will learn to:

> * copy the contents of cells
>
> * point to cells
>
> * use absolute references
>
> * move cells about

This lesson is about what is probably the most useful feature of SuperCalc, and in fact of all spreadsheet programs. When you have completed it you will find that you can create large sheets very quickly by copying the contents of one or more cells into different parts of the sheet.

■ COPYING CELLS AND USING POINT MODE

Earlier versions of SuperCalc called this operation "Replication" which although an ugly word conveys the idea behind what is happening very well. It is of particular use when you need to have the same formula in more than one cell, especially when it is a complex formula that takes a lot of keystrokes to enter. But we will do a simple one first.

	Action	*Result*
1.	Key in **/LA:EX2 (Ret) A** or Key in **/LB:EX2 (Ret) A**	Loads the spreadsheet **EX2.CAL** and displays it on the screen.
2.	Highlight cell B4.	
3.	Key in **/C** (Copy command)	**From? Enter range or *graph-range**

Note that you are in **POINT** mode now - see the bottom of the screen. This means that you can move the highlight about and its position is reflected in the cell range displayed in the status line.

	Action	*Result*
4.	Highlight cell B5.	**From?(Enter Range)** **9>/Copy,B5**
5.	Press . (Start of range is B5)	Anchor cell.

	Action		Result
6.	Highlight cell D6.		**From?(Enter Range)** **12>/Copy,B5:D6**
7.	Press **(Ret)** (Range now defined as B5:D6)		**To?(Enter Cell);then <RETURN> or <,>** **for Options**
8.	Highlight cell E5.		
9.	Press **(Ret)** (Start of copied range defined as E5)		A copy of the contents of cells B5:D6 is copied into the range E5:G6.
10.	Key in **/GF**(Global command, Formula option)		Displays the contents of the cells.

Now try this again and copy the contents of the block of cells B9:D12 to a new block starting at E9. You can now enter additional data in cells E2:G4 and E8:G8 in order to get the following.

	A		B		C		D		E		F		G	
1														
2			January		February		March		April		May		June	
3	Wages		440		440		440		440		460		460	
4	Tips		85		75		98		90		88		95	
5	Bonus		12%B3		12%C3		12%D3		12%E3		12%F3		12%G3	
6	Total		B3+B4+B5		C3+C4+C5		D3+D4+D5		E3+E4+E5		F3+F4+F5		G3+G4+G5	
7			---------		---------		---------		---------		---------		---------	
8	Expenses		125		143		110		126		130		150	
9	Tax		20%B8		20%C8		20%D8		20%E8		20%F8		20%G8	
10	Total		B8+B9		C8+C9		D8+D9		E8+E9		F8+F9		G8+G9	
11			=========		=========		=========		=========		=========		=========	
12	Net Pay		B6-B10		C6-C10		D6-D10		E6-E10		F6-F10		G6-G10	
13														

Return to a conventional display first by using **/GF**. When you have completed this new sheet, save it away on disk under the name **EX3**.

Now try this.

	Action		Result
11.	Key in **/ZY** (Zap command - Yes)		The screen contents are zapped.
12.	Highlight cell A1.		
13.	Key in **100 (Ret)**		**100** in cell A1.
14.	Highlight cell A2.		
15.	Key in **A1+10 (Ret)**		**110** in cell A2.
16.	Key in **/C** (Copy command)		**From? Enter range or *graph-range**